FASCINATING WEXFOI

C000221671

Fascinating Wexford History

VOLUME THREE

A collection of more intriguing stories
from County Wexford's past.

DES KIELY

PARSIFAL PRESS

Published by the Parsifal Press, Newry
Copyright © 2021 by Des Kiely

A CIP record for this title is available from The British Library

ISBN: 978-1-9196324-0-7

All rights reserved.

Without limiting the rights under copyright reserved above,
no part of this publication may be reproduced, stored in or introduced
into a retrieval system, or transmitted, in any
form or by any means (electronic, mechanical, photocopying,
recording or otherwise), without the prior permission
of the publisher.

The author has made every reasonable effort to contact the copyright
holders of photographs and texts reproduced in this book.
The publisher apologizes for any errors or omissions and would be
grateful if notified of any corrections that should be incorporated
in future reprints or editions of this book.

Special thanks to Katherine Carroll, Chris Courtney,
Michael Dempsey, Gráinne Doran, Pat Doyle,
Yvonne Hadden, Mark and Emma Hewlett,
David M. Kiely, Michael Murphy and James O'Connor

Photo credits:
Cork Examiner, Tony Crosbie, Paddy Donovan, Frank Doyle,
Ger Hore, Irish Times, National Gallery of Ireland,
National Library of Ireland, Dawn Ward

Cover art and design by the author
Set in 10.5 Iowan Old Style by the author

For my grandchildren
Seán and Faye

ABOUT THE AUTHOR

Des Kiely is by profession a graphic designer living in Wexford. He can trace his family history back to the village of Stradbally in County Waterford and to the house where his great-great-great grandfather John Kiely was born in 1778. The family moved north to Derry and again back  south to Dublin, then Wicklow, so Des has almost completed the journey back home to Waterford. His hobbies include photography, music, art and writing local history. This is his fourth book on Wexford history, the first three being his bestsellers *Famous Wexford People in History* and *Fascinating Wexford History, Volumes One and Two*.

CONTENTS

FOREWORD

Thomas Jefferson said: "I like the dreams of the future better than the history of the past". But our story defines ourselves – to know the struggles, triumphs, failures, and experiences of those generations who lived in our place, gives us roots and understanding upon which we build our future dreams.

Des Kiely in his series *Fascinating Wexford History*, again and again opens windows into individual stories of our past. Stories of the absurd to the tragic. Of the chaos of nation building to the experience of an earlier pandemic.

One chapter especially draws my attention. Not surprisingly it is the story of the epic struggle of Wexford workers between August 1911 and February 1912 – the Lockout. I have been told the tales of that time, passed down with pride by families whose members lived it. It was a truly defining period for Wexford town, which set its industrial policy and indeed its politics for a century after. On the 17th February 1912, over 5,000 Wexford men and women gathered in the Faythe to cheer James Connolly and the courage and steadfastness of Wexford workers. After many months of arduous resistance, a settlement had been brokered by Connolly and others after the imprisonment of I.T.G.W.U. organizer P.T. Daly. Within a few short years, Connolly as Commandment General of the Army of the Irish Republic would be executed for his part in the 1916 Rising.

Des in each of his stand-alone detailed insights builds the foundations of our history, sets out the flow of our everchanging story.

In this place we call home, this South East corner of Ireland, we can trace the migration of people and the evolution of our society back well over a thousand years. We are the products of all who went before us. Culture like identity is enriched by embracing the new and remembering the old.

Des Kiely continues to play an invaluable role in chronicling the mosaic of our past that is truly fascinating.

Brendan Howlin TD

Killanne woman hanged in London for gruesome murder

The killer Catherine Lawler.   *The victim, her employer Julia Thomas.*

KILLANNE, the small crossroads community about seven miles west of Enniscorthy, produced 1798 rebel leader John Kelly, and in more recent times gave hurling the legendary Rackard brothers. In the intervening years a woman born in the area would go on to be hanged for committing one of the most notorious murders of the Victorian era in London. In 1879, the County Wexford maid killed the mistress of the house, dismembered her body and disposed of it in various places around the city. It would be 2010 before her skull was found on the property of the renowned naturalist, Sir David Attenborough.

Catherine Lawler was born into poor circumstances in Killanne in 1849, the final year of the Great Famine. From a young age she was in trouble with the law, having to resort to theft to survive. In 1864 she appeared in court in Gorey on charges of stealing items of clothing from shops in New Ross and Enniscorthy. As prisoner number 235, Catherine Lawler's age was recorded in the Register of Prisoners in Wexford as 19. She was jailed then for twelve months for the theft of a plaid dress. Catherine was described as a '...strongly-made woman of about 5 feet 4 inches in height with sallow and much freckled complexion and prominent front teeth.'

Having stolen money to pay for her fare, she sailed for Liverpool in 1867, and on arrival continued to steal to survive. The following February, now in her early twenties, she was sentenced to four years' penal servitude for committing larceny in the city. On release in 1872, Catherine moved on to London, where she took cleaning jobs in various parts of the city and was continually stealing from her employers. In Notting Hill, while working as a domestic servant, she met a man named John Strong, who she moved in with, and he became her accomplice in further robberies. She became pregnant by him and gave birth to a son who she registered as John Webster in April 1874, before Stone abandoned her. She later claimed that he forced her into crime, as stated: *'I was forsaken by him, and committed crimes for the purpose of supporting myself and child.'* Catherine named three different men at various times as the father and claimed she had once been married to a sailor named Webster, but this was never verified.

Catherine moved from one boarding house to another, selling off items of furniture from her room and moving on to repeat the crime elsewhere. She used various aliases, including Webster, Webb and Gibbs, as well as her real name, Lawler, in order to evade arrest. But when the police caught up with her in 1875 she was sentenced to 18 months in Wandsworth Prison, having been charged with 39 counts of larceny and again in 1877 to 12 months for

The house of Julia Thomas on the left, scene of the murder in 1879, and The Hole in the Wall public house two doors up can be seen on the extreme right.

theft. A cleaning lady named Sarah Crease with whom she had become friends found herself caring for young John during his mother's spells in prison.

Now known as Catherine or Kate Webster, she stood in as a cleaner for the Loder family in Richmond when Crease fell ill. In January 1879, Lucy Loder recommended Catherine to a friend, Julia Thomas, who lived at Mayfield Cottages on Park Road, whom she knew to be in need of a domestic servant. Julia Thomas (née Batterbee) was a former schoolteacher who had been twice widowed and was now in her 50s. She was known to be a little eccentric, with an 'excitable temperament' and therefore unable to keep a servant employed for long. The pair met and Mrs Thomas engaged Catherine immediately, without making enquiries into her past or her character. However, soon Catherine's new employer was criticizing the standard of her work, her timekeeping and regular drunkenness. Their relationship soon deteriorated. Catherine Webster later said: *'At first I thought her a nice old lady...but...when I had finished my work in my rooms, she used to go over it again after me, and point out places where she said I did not clean, showing evidence of a nasty spirit towards me.'* Julia Thomas finally decided to dismiss Catherine and gave her notice to leave on Friday, 28 February. The last entry that Julia recorded in her diary was: 'Gave Catherine warning to leave'.

However, Catherine could not find other work or accommodation by that date and she persuaded Mrs Thomas to allow her to stay until after the weekend. Catherine had Sunday afternoons off and she would visit her four-year-old son John, who was being cared for by Sarah Crease. Mrs Thomas attended Presbyterian service at the Lecture Hall every Sunday and Catherine needed to be home in good time to help her prepare to go out. But Catherine stopped off at the Hole in the Wall pub, located just two doors up from the house, and this delayed Mrs Thomas's departure. When Catherine finally returned home the two women quarrelled. Witnesses at the Lecture Hall noted that Mrs Thomas had been in an agitated state when she arrived and would later say that she left before the end of the service.

When Julia Thomas returned home she went straight upstairs. Catherine followed her and another argument ensued. In a fit of temper, Catherine pushed Mrs Thomas down the stairs and she fell hard on the hall floor below. Afraid that she might start screaming and therefore attract attention from the neighbours, Catherine caught her by the throat and strangled her.

Elizabeth Ives, the next-door neighbour and landlady of Mrs Thomas, later recalled hearing what she described as being like a chair falling over, but no sounds of quarrelling.

Next, Catherine wanted to get rid of the body and in her confession later stated: *'I determined to do away with the body as best I could. I chopped the head from the body with the assistance of a razor which I used to cut through the flesh afterwards. I also used the meat saw and the carving knife to cut the body up with. I prepared the copper with water to boil the body to prevent identity; and as soon as I had succeeded in cutting it up I placed it in the copper and boiled it. I opened the stomach with the carving knife, and burned up as much of the parts as I could.'* She also confessed to being *'greatly overcome both by the sight before me and the smell.'* She said she tried to sell the fat, rendered from boiling Julia's body, to a local restaurant. When that didn't work she claimed that she *'fed it to some young boys, who ate two bowls full.'*

Over the next few days, Catherine put on an air of normality to neighbours while she attempted to pack the victim's body into a holdall and her head into a wooden hatbox. However, she was unable to fit all parts of the corpse into the bag and so she buried the head in a shallow grave in the stables behind the Hole in the Wall pub. Catherine threw the hatbox, filled with body parts, off Richmond Bridge and into the Thames. She continued into Twickenham, where she disposed of one of the feet on a rubbish heap. Two days later the hatbox was found washed up about five miles downstream under Barnes Railway Bridge in Hounslow, in shallow water by the river bank. The police were summoned and a murder investigation was now underway. The unidentified remains were buried in an unmarked plot in Barnes Cemetery, and the case soon became known as the 'Barnes Mystery'.

Catherine needed cash and began selling off furniture from the house as well as Julia's jewellery and the gold fillings from her teeth. She found a buyer for the furniture from the house; John Church, the landlord of The Rising Sun public house in Hammersmith. By now neighbours were becoming increasingly concerned about the whereabouts of Mrs Thomas. When two horse-drawn wagons arrived to remove the furniture on 18 March, the landlady Miss Ives enquired of one of the men as to who had ordered the removal of the goods. The man stated that Mrs Thomas had done so, thereby indicating Catherine to be Mrs Thomas. Catherine, realizing she had been exposed, promptly fled. The police were called and on examination of the

The former RIC barracks at Killanne crossroads.
(photo: Des Kiely)

house found bloodstains and charred finger bones in the fireplace. They also discovered a letter that showed her old home address back in Killanne. Scotland Yard put out a nationwide alert to find Catherine Webster or Lawler.

She made her way by train from King's Cross station to Liverpool with her young son and boarded a steamship back to Ireland. They arrived at her uncle's house, situated about two miles from Killanne, on 21 March. RIC head constable, Patrick O'Callaghan of Wexford police station, alerted Killanne barracks by telegram a week later to be on the lookout for Catherine Lawler. Sergeant Bill Roche remembered arresting her for stealing fifteen years earlier and so he and Constable Hackett checked the house of her uncle, where they found her and her little boy. She claimed that her name was Kate Webster but they arrested her and took her to Killanne barracks.

Two Scotland Yard detectives arrived in Enniscorthy on Friday 28 March and met Sergeant Roche at Enniscorthy barracks, where Catherine was now being held. According to *The People* newspaper, reporting on the events of 29 March, Catherine Lawler '...*was conveyed by the Dublin, Wicklow and Wexford Railway from the Enniscorthy station at one o'clock today, on her route to England, in charge of Inspectors Jones and Dowdall, of the English Detective Service'*. They arrived at Harcourt Street Station terminus and she was taken to Exchange Street police station.

That night they travelled on the mail boat out of Kingstown to Holyhead, arriving at Euston Station in London at seven o'clock on Sunday morning. On their journey back to England, the accused woman stated to Inspector Dowdall that the perpetrator of the crime was in fact John Church, the owner of The Rising Sun pub in Hammersmith. She said that she had kept company with the man for several years but according to *The People* newspaper, '*she introduced him into Mrs Thomas's house, and represented him as her brother; he proposed to her to do away with Mrs Thomas by poison or otherwise for her money, and live with him, as he was tired of his own "old woman".'*

On arrival in London, Catherine was brought to Richmond police station. John Church was also taken into custody and on 1 April, they were both charged before Richmond Magistrates' Court with murder. The pre-trial hearings attracted huge crowds as had the murder scene at Park Road after the crime was discovered and made public.

The trial at the Old Bailey, which opened on 2 July 1879, lasted for six days and was followed in detail by

From a poster announcing the trial and execution of Catherine Lawler, aka Kate Webster.

the newspapers. Catherine, when asked, claimed she was aged 'about 30' though she may have been older. She protested her innocence throughout and attempted to blame the murder on John Church. Finally, she accepted responsibility but tried to convince the court that other people, including the absent father of her child, had forced her to commit the crime. In the end the jury took two hours to find Catherine guilty of the wilful and premeditated murder of Julia Thomas. When asked by the judge if there was a reason why she should not be executed, she insisted that she was pregnant. But following an examination by a physician it was confirmed that this too was a lie. The judge sentenced her to death and she was returned to nearby Newgate Prison.

On 28 July, the day before her execution, Catherine was transferred to Wandsworth Prison, where she had spent time before working for Mrs Thomas. There she wrote a formal confession to her solicitor in the presence of the prison governor and a Catholic priest, Father McEnrey, who attended her. In it she described in detail how she alone committed the murder, got rid of the body parts and even how she removed the head.

The Wexford native was hanged the next day at 9am in the 'execution shed' – a building separate from the main prison. Public hangings had been outlawed eleven years previously. According to the press, she *'walked to the scaffold without assistance. She appeared penitent and resigned. She had a drop of six feet, and died apparently without a struggle.'* The prison bell began to toll at a quarter to nine. At three minutes past nine a crowd that had gathered outside the prison gate cheered as a black flag was hoisted over the prison walls, indicating that the death sentence had been carried out. The hangman, William Marwood, had himself developed the 'long drop' technique that would have caused instantaneous death. Her remains were buried in an unmarked grave in the prison's grounds and the coffin was filled with quicklime – believed to speed up the decay process.

Even before her trial began, Madame Tussaud's had a waxwork of the 'Richmond Murderess' on display. *The Freeman's Journal* in Dublin described the case as *'one of the most sensational and awful chapters in the annals of human wickedness.'* There was already much prejudice towards the Irish who had emigrated to England after the Famine. The outrageous crime committed by Catherine Lawler fitted with the public perception of the Irish in much of Victorian England that associated them with drunkenness and criminality. Catherine was the subject of a souvenir edition of *The Illustrated Police News* as well as many ballads and books. It was claimed that Barnes Cemetery was haunted by a ghostly nun that would hover over where Julia Thomas's body parts were buried. On the day after the execution, an auction was held at the former home of Julia Thomas where she was murdered. John Church managed to acquire her furniture after all, along with the knife that Catherine Webster used to dismember her body. The house stood unoccupied for nearly twenty years as nobody wished to live there.

POSTSCRIPT

In 1952, over seventy years after the crime, a young television producer at the BBC named David Attenborough and his wife Jane bought the house situated between the notorious house of Mrs Thomas and the Hole in the Wall pub. They reared their family there and Attenborough remained living at the address after the death of his wife in 1997. When the pub closed in 2007 it was left to fall derelict and Attenborough feared it might be replaced with a block of flats, right on his doorstep. So the famous naturalist and wildlife broadcaster bought it for £1 million in 2009. *'I wouldn't say I am rescuing it, but the front will be retained'*, explained Sir David, much to the delight of residents in the upmarket Richmond area, who include Mick Jagger, Pete Townshend and, at the time, his older brother – the late film director Richard Attenborough.

Sir David Attenborough outside his home on Park Road, Richmond in southwest London, with the Hole in the Wall pub, where Julia Thomas's skull was discovered in 2010, on the right.

When builders moved in the following year to carry out excavation work, they uncovered a 'dark circular object'. It was found beneath foundations that had been laid in the 1960s on the site of the pub's old stable buildings at the rear. This turned out to be a woman's skull, found buried above a layer of Victorian tiles. It was immediately speculated that the skull was that of Julia Thomas, whose head was never found after her corpse was dismembered 130 years earlier. Richmond police were immediately notified and after carbon dating was carried out at the University of Edinburgh, the skull was found to be no more recent than 1880. Fracture marks were consistent with Catherine Lawler's account of having thrown Mrs Thomas down the stairs. It was also found to have depleted collagen levels, consistent with having been boiled. A DNA test was not possible because no relatives of Thomas could be traced and there was no record of where exactly the rest of her body had been buried. At an inquest held in 2011 the coroner declared: *'Putting all the circumstantial evidence together there is clear, convincing and compelling evidence that this is the skull of Julia Thomas.'*

The shattered skull of murder victim Julia Thomas, found over 130 years after the crime.

Nazi spy landed near Ballycullane led to cracking top secret code

Des Kiely

Günther Schütz was dropped in Yoletown near Ballycullane, one night in March 1941, thinking he was near Newbridge, County Kildare.

THROUGHOUT the 1930s, those who remained in the IRA following the Civil War continued to be hostile to the Irish Free State and the existence of Northern Ireland. Under Seán Russell, they declared war on Britain in 1939 and a bombing campaign was carried out in England in the months before the outbreak of the Second World War. The IRA looked to Nazi Germany to supply them with weapons, ammunition and explosives and meetings took place between them and the German envoy in Ireland, Dr Eduard Hempel, and other members of the Nazi party. Hempel was posted as Minister to Ireland in 1937 and held the post throughout the war, until 1945.

Germany was keen that De Valera's government remained neutral during the war. De Valera denied Britain the use of Irish ports, control of which they had retained until 1938. The other reason for Germany cooperating with the IRA was to divert British resources from the war, in the event of a nationalist rebellion in Northern Ireland.

By 1940, the British recognized that Germany was planning to invade Britain. They believed that Ireland might be occupied in advance or possibly during an invasion of Britain itself as a diversionary attack. *Unternehmen Grün* (Operation Green) was Nazi Germany's plan to invade the south coast of

Ireland. Fearing Germany might carry out its threat, an Irish-British plan was devised whereby Northern Ireland was to become a base for British troops, who would cross the border, at the invitation of the Irish Government, to repel the German invaders. However, Hitler declared that 'Éire's neutrality must be respected. A neutral Irish Free State is of greater value to us than a hostile Ireland'.

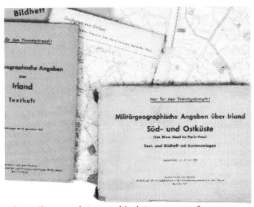

The 'Military and Geographical Assessment of Ireland' ran to five volumes, produced by German High Command in preparation for 'Operation Green' – the possible invasion of Ireland.

Germany ran about a dozen agents into Ireland during the war, but most were discovered and imprisoned. Hermann Görtz, a trained German military intelligence officer, was probably the most important. He parachuted into the country, in full military uniform, landing at Ballivor, County Meath in May 1940. Görtz handed over more than £100,000 to the IRA, and during his eighteen months evading capture he passed information about Irish military and coastal defences back to the *Abwehr* (German military intelligence). When he was finally arrested Görtz was first held in Arbour Hill Prison. After his release from Athlone in 1946 he planned to remain in Ireland. However, he was re-arrested the following year and was about to be deported to Germany to face trial for espionage. While in the Aliens Office in Dublin Castle, he committed suicide by swallowing cyanide. He was buried in full Luftwaffe uniform, his coffin draped in a swastika flag, in Deansgrange Cemetery.

DROPPED OVER WEXFORD

A year after flying to Ireland carrying Görtz, who was then still at large, Luftwaffe pilot Lt Gartenfeld departed Schiphol Airport in the Netherlands, which was under German occupation, on the night of 12-13 March 1941. His passenger on board the Heinkel He -111 bomber this time was 29-year-old Sergeant Günther Schütz. His mission was to parachute into Ireland, where he was to report back to the *Abwehr* on economic and military movements on both sides of the border. He was also instructed to radio daily weather reports to the Luftwaffe. Schütz carried with him a fake South African passport in the name of Hans Marschner, a substantial amount of cash, a transmitter, a microscope and an ingenious coding system for encrypting messages – believed by the Germans to be unbreakable.

Flying over England, they encountered severe gunfire as they were picked up by searchlights. Gartenfeld lost altitude as he flew over what he believed must be Liverpool and successfully reached the Irish Sea. When they entered Irish airspace he cut off the engines at 6,500 feet and Schütz prepared his parachute. The plan was to drop Schütz close to Newbridge, County Kildare. From there he was to travel to a safe house on Merrion Square in Dublin. But Gartenfeld had no way of knowing where he was as he navigated by instruments only. Schütz leaped into the darkness and drifted silently towards Irish soil. As soon as he landed he concealed his parachute and jump helmet beneath the bank of a nearby stream.

His map and compass were of little use as he found the nearest road and wandered aimlessly along in the dark. Signposts had been removed at the outbreak of the war, lest enemy forces use them for navigation. However, as dawn broke, Schütz happened upon a sign indicating 'New Ross 10 miles'. Checking his map, he found he was more than 60 miles south of his planned landing zone and that they must have flown over South Wales, not Liverpool.

He decided to head in the direction of Wexford town, where he might catch a bus to Dublin and continued walking along the quiet country road, carrying his suitcase containing the vital transmitter. After a short while, a young female on a bicycle passed and they greeted one another. Meanwhile, the woman, who was employed in Carrickbyrne Garda Station, reported her sighting of the stranger to the gardaí.

Two gardaí on bicycles went in search and spotted the outsider as he attempted to take cover in a ditch at Poulpeasty, on the old New Ross to Wexford road. They questioned him as to where he was heading and Schütz said

A scene from the RTÉ drama series 'Caught In A Free State' (1983), portraying the arrest of Günther Schütz by local gardaí at Poulpeasty.

his car had broken down on his way to New Ross. He claimed his name was Hans Marschner and was a South African national. 'That's a fine suitcase you've got there,' said one of the gardaí. 'In the haberdashery business?' 'Yes,' replied Schütz. They asked him to open it and were amazed to see its contents: the radio transmitter, a microscope and a lot of cash. As he was handcuffed, Schütz knew his mission was over, just hours after landing on Irish soil.

The gardaí walked him back to Camaross, the nearest village, where he enjoyed some Guinness and sandwiches in Rochford's pub. Meanwhile, garda reinforcements from Wexford arrived in a squad car. As the German spy was led away, he asked 'What will happen to me?' 'Don't worry, we'll hang you, that's all,' one of the gardaí chuckled. Unfamiliar with Irish sarcasm, the prisoner went pale. They drove him to Ballycullane where he had buried his parachute and he handed it over, along with his jump suit and helmet. Before leaving Wexford, the gardaí made a list of his possessions, including a photograph of an unknown gentleman, and passed this on to G2 – the Irish Military Intelligence Service. He was then driven to the Bridewell Garda Station in Dublin and from there to Arbour Hill Prison.

In prison, 'Marschner' was questioned by G2, and Dr Richard Hayes. A great linguist, Hayes was Director of the National Library of Ireland and also headed up the cryptography unit of the Irish Defence Forces. During the Second World War, the quiet-spoken but wily librarian would become the country's top codebreaker. He was also an impressive interrogator of German spies, who knew him only as 'Captain Grey'. Hayes entered the spy's cell and immediately addressed the prisoner in German. Schütz admitted to being a German agent but not to his true identity and when questioned about the microscope, he claimed to be a keen stamp collector. 'G'way, you didn't bring a microscope all the way from Germany to examine stamps,' said Hayes.

BREAKING THE CODE

Hayes had already broken a complex letter-based code used by Hermann Görtz in his cable messages from Ireland to the *Abwehr*. This had baffled Britain's MI5 and cryptologists at Bletchley Park. The first of Görtz's messages that he unlocked used the key 'Cathleen Ni Houlihan'.

'Marschner' had a number of newspaper clippings tucked into his pocket book, which intrigued Hayes. At first they appeared innocuous until Hayes

Dr Richard Hayes, the brilliant codebreaker, who cracked the German microdot code carried by Günther Schütz.

used the confiscated microscope to examine one of the articles. To his amazement, when viewed at 400 times magnification, he discovered messages hidden in microdots within three letter 'O's in the text. He found more microdots in random characters in the newspaper cuttings. The secreted messages were not even encoded and within ten days Richard Hayes had found and translated thirty pages of the German agent's instructions and an extensive list of contacts in Ireland. The microdots were a closely guarded 'top secret' in Germany and Schütz's whole mission was now rendered obsolete. Schütz was dumbfounded and explained that the idea of the microdots was conceived by scientists attached to the *Abwehr* to replace the use of invisible ink and that he was the first agent to travel outside Germany to employ them.

Hayes made daily visits to 'Hans Marschner' in jail and soon deduced Marschner's true identity to be that of Günther Schütz. His handwriting matched letters written to Hermann Görtz that were signed 'G. Schütz'. G2 identified the mystery man in the photograph found with Schütz as Werner Unland, a German sleeper agent who had arrived with his wife before the war and used his apartment at 46 Merrion Square, Dublin as a base for spying. Schütz had been instructed to make his way to Unland after landing in County Kildare. This led to the arrest of Unland and his wife as they strolled along Clare Street in Dublin in April 1941. He too was held in Arbour Hill Prison.

ESCAPE FROM MOUNTJOY

After a further month's detention, Schütz was transferred to Sligo, where he spent eight weeks in solitary confinement. He was then moved to Mountjoy Prison in Dublin, where he applied himself to planning his escape. He made the acquaintance of a number of IRA inmates who supplied him with two hacksaw blades. He also befriended a republican-minded prison guard who procured a fur coat, a dress, silk stockings, shoes, a wig, headscarf and make-up. Schütz explained to the governor, Seán Kavanagh, that they were gifts for his girlfriend back in Germany, and this was accepted. Along with a Dutch prisoner, Jan van Loon, who had offered his services as a spy to the German Legation in Dublin, an escape plan was hatched.

Schütz painstakingly filed through the bars of his cell until he and Van Loon finally broke through on 15 February 1942. They jumped 23 feet to the ground but while scaling the prison wall using curtain rope, Van Loon fell and Schütz had no choice but to leave him behind. He made his way, dressed in women's clothing, to the Drumcondra home of one of the IRA prisoners: James O'Hanlon. Posters soon appeared around the city

Dr Eduard Hempel, Nazi Germany's envoy in Ireland (1937-45), pictured in Dublin in 1938.

offering a £500 reward for the capture of 'Hans Marschner'. The German envoy, Eduard Hempel, denied having any knowledge of the spy. But secretly he had notified Berlin of Schütz's escape and was instructed to get word to him that he was to continue his mission in Ireland and to supply him with sufficient cash to fund it.

Through Joe O'Hanlon, a brother of James, Schütz made contact with Caitlín Brugha, who agreed to pass messages to Hempel on his behalf. He requested that he return to Germany, possibly by U-boat. Hempel, however, feared that if Schütz was caught trying to flee the country, it could jeopardize Germany's diplomatic mission to Ireland. He informed the *Abwehr*, who declared any assistance to aid Schütz's escape was to be denied. Hempel instead was to tell Schütz that a new transmitter would be sent to him, possibly to be dropped by parachute.

Caitlín Brugha (born Kathleen Kingston) married the republican activist Cathal Brugha in 1912. Brugha (born Charles Burgess), a partner in Lalor Candles, was a former Chief of Staff of the IRA and appointed Minister for Defence in 1919. He was anti-Treaty and was shot by Free State troops in O'Connell Street at the outbreak of the Civil War in 1922 and died two days later. Caitlín ran for her husband's Sinn Féin seat in the Waterford constituency in the 1923 general election. She topped the poll, beating William Redmond, son of Wexford politician John Redmond, into second place. In 1924, Caitlín, widowed with six children under the age of 10, founded the well-known Dublin menswear business, Kingston's, with branches on O'Connell Street, Grafton Street and George's Street. The brand is remembered for its advertising slogan: *'A Kingston shirt makes all the difference'*.

Schütz moved between various addresses, arranged by Caitlín, over the next six weeks. Initially staying with a couple named Cowman in Blackrock, she had him moved in the dead of night to her own house in exclusive Temple Gardens, Rathmines. Caitlín asked him in return to help secure arms and ammunition from Germany for the IRA. Members of the Belfast IRA offered to arrange a boat to take him to Brest in German-occupied Brittany. Charles McGuinness, an adventurer and German collaborator from Derry, was to be the boat's captain. But McGuinness was arrested in Cork, having obtained an Irish Navy organizational chart that he was planning to pass on to Hempel, and was interned for the rest of the war. He drowned in 1947 off Ballymoney, County Wexford when his schooner, bound for the Caribbean, ran aground.

Caitlín Brugha (born Kathleen Kingston), the widow of Cathal Brugha, harboured Günther Schütz at her home in Dublin.

During his stay in Caitlín Brugha's house, Schütz composed coded messages to be sent via Hempel to the *Abwehr*. He was also messaging the Northern IRA, but these were being monitored by Richard Hayes and the listening station in Collins Barracks. Hayes successfully broke the cipher that Schütz was using and was able to inform G2 of the content of his messages.

The IRA got word to Schütz that they had a boat waiting in Bray to take him to Germany. On 30 April 1942, he waited to be picked up from Brugha's house in Rathmines, dressed in female clothes and in full make-up. Caitlín's daughter answered the door, not to IRA members as she expected, but two G2 officers accompanied by the gardaí, who promptly arrested Schütz. They also raided Kingston's shop and arrested Caitlín Brugha.

Back in Mountjoy, Schütz was kept in solitary confinement for two months. Hempel had alerted Berlin of Schütz's earlier escape and, although he was ultimately caught, he was promoted in his absence to lieutenant. Schütz was moved to a section dedicated to captured German spies. He was held alongside Werner Unland and others and they lived in relative comfort and freedom, but all their outgoing mail was censored. Eventually all ten captured German agents were moved out of Dublin to a newly constructed internment camp at Costume Barracks in Athlone. Eduard Hempel informed Berlin of the conditions in which the men were being held and he was instructed to secretly have a £25 monthly allowance paid to each prisoner. Lieutenant Schütz and the other German internees spent the remainder of the war in Athlone.

When news that Adolf Hitler had shot himself at his bunker in Berlin on 30 April 1945, the Taoiseach, Éamon de Valera, called to Hempel's home in Dún Laoghaire two days later to express his condolences. The visit caused outrage around the world. De Valera wrote to his friend, Wexford-born Robert Brennan, the Irish envoy in Washington: *"to have failed to call upon the German representative would have been an act of unpardonable discourtesy to the German nation and to Dr Hempel. During the whole of the war, Dr Hempel's conduct was irreproachable. ... I certainly was not going to add to his humiliation in the hour of defeat."*

On 10 September 1946, all ten German internees were informed that they were being given 'leave from camp' and the right of asylum. Schütz moved to Dublin and in May 1947 married a nurse, Una Mackey, whom he had been courting while in Athlone. In the same year, he was flown from Baldonnel to Frankfurt and taken to a US Army interrogation camp near Oberursel but was soon released.

He and his wife settled in Hamburg for a number of years before returning to Ireland in the 1960s. They ran the Clogga Bay Hotel near Arklow for a time and eventually retired to their home in Avoca. Günther Schütz died in his sleep on New Year's Day 1991 in Shankill, County Dublin, aged 78.

Günther Schütz, aged about 70, photographed in 1983 with the German actor Götz Burger, who portrayed him in the television drama 'Caught In A Free State'.
(photo: RTÉ Archives)

Michael Collins' defiant rally in divided Wexford town

Collins spoke from the steps of Cousins' Mineral Water premises in St Peter's Square, Wexford in April 1922.

FOUR MONTHS before he was assassinated in his home county of Cork, Michael Collins, then Minister for Finance in the independent Irish Free State, visited Wexford town. It was a turbulent period in Irish history. Wexford, like the rest of the country, was torn apart by pro- and anti-Treaty factions in the lead-up to the General Election in June 1922 that would result in the outbreak of the Civil War. Anti-Treaty IRA activists were determined to spoil his planned political rally in St Peter's Square.

Michael Collins was scheduled to arrive in Wexford on Saturday, 8 April 1922 and his speech was planned for the following day. *The People* newspaper ran notices in their Friday edition announcing special trains to Wexford and one issued by the Wexford police warning: *'The sale of intoxicating liquors to any person whatever on that day is forbidden.'*

The train carrying Collins and his entourage steamed into Wexford train station on the Saturday night to the sounds of exploding fog signals announcing his arrival. They were met by a reception committee and as the party emerged from the station there was cheering from the large crowd that had gathered on Redmond Place. On arrival at the Talbot Hotel, Michael Collins was presented with a case of Irish-made smoking pipes, which he was known to be fond of. This was presented to him by Bridgetown nationalist

Group photograph taken outside Pierce's Foundry offices on 9 April 1922. Front row (l to r): William Hearn (Wexford Engineering), Mayor Richard Corish, Philip Pierce (Pierce's), Michael Collins, William and Andrew Doyle (Selskar Ironworks) and possibly T.W. Salmon (Pierce's). (photo: Charles Vize)

Kathleen Browne, accompanied by Mary Furlong, Maeve Gregory and Mrs M. O'Connor of the recently formed Cumann na Saoirse. This was a breakaway military group that had taken the side of the Treaty and split from the anti-Treaty organization, Cumann na mBan.

The following morning, Collins attended 11 o'clock Mass in the Franciscan Friary, accompanied by the mayor, Richard Corish, local businessman J.J. Stafford and others. He then called on the mother of Matthew Furlong on South Main Street. Furlong had died from injuries he received when testing a mortar in County Meath in 1920, intended for use in attacks on RIC barracks.

It was then on to the Mill Road Iron Works (Pierce's), where he was given a tour by Philip Pierce and the foundry manager, T. W. Salmon. The group photograph above appeared in the local press and was credited to local photographer Charles Vize. With studios on South Main Street, and Slaney Street in Enniscorthy,

Posing outside Pierce's with a Pierce bicycle, presented to him on the day of his visit. The photograph was discovered in Pierce's in 1967.

Vize was also manager of the Cinema Palace. Collins posed with local politicians and the proprietors of the other two major foundries in the town – Selskar Ironworks and Wexford Engineering (Star Ironworks). Sitting in the front row among the business elite was the Mayor, Richard Corish, who had been blacklisted by all three foundries following the Lockout of 1911.

RAIL AND ROAD DISRUPTION

Meanwhile, chaos ensued on the railway routes and roads into Wexford from Dublin, Waterford and New Ross on the Sunday morning. The special trains were disrupted by anti-Treaty IRA members intent on preventing or delaying people reaching Wexford to attend Collins' speech, scheduled for 3pm. Roads were blocked by felled trees.

The train from Dublin, carrying about a thousand people, was forced to stop at Woodenbridge, County Wicklow, where tracks on the bridge crossing the Avoca river had been torn up. The passengers were forced to disembark while workmen attempted to repair the damaged line. They were delayed by armed men, who threw some of their tools into the river below. When a local man protested on the station platform, he was immediately surrounded by men armed with rifles and revolvers and forced to apologize on his knees. Eventually, the train continued as far as Enniscorthy, where the driver was removed from his cab by activists. A number of journalists who were travelling

Workmen carrying out repairs to damaged railway tracks on 9 April 1922. (photo: Pathé)

on the train continued their journey to Wexford in cars, encountering felled trees blocking the road they were taking. Finally reaching Wexford at around 6pm, five hours later than scheduled, the exasperated passengers had missed the public meeting.

Felling trees to block roads was a simple but effective tactic used by the anti-Treaty IRA. (photo: Waterford County Museum)

The Waterford to Rosslare train was forced to stop between Bridgetown and Killinick, having encountered damaged railway tracks. Repairs were quickly carried out but it was then discovered that telegraph wires had been cut and so the onward journey had to be cancelled. This also held up the Cork to Rosslare express.

Railway tracks on the Waterford to New Ross line were removed near Aylwardstown, causing delays. At New Ross station, the driver and stoker of the special train heading to Wexford were removed by armed men and driven some distance outside the town in a car. About seventy passengers who had purchased tickets were refunded their fares by the stationmaster. Word came through that the line towards Rathgarogue was blocked in any event.

The New Ross to Wexford road was made impassable at Arnestown by a large tree. Captain Paddy Mackey of the South Wexford Brigade, who were emphatically anti-Treaty, was helped by others to cut away the obstruction with saws. They drove towards Wexford carrying their implements but found no more trees blocking the route. Mackey disapproved of the blocking of roads and holding up trains and claimed they were not carried out under instructions from the South Wexford Brigade. He also complained that the motor car belonging to Fred Taylor, a New Ross vet from 1894 to 1944, had been commandeered. In a statement later to the *New Ross Standard*, Paddy Mackey stated that he believed in freedom of speech for all sides. He said that in his opinion *'such methods were calculated to advance the Treaty cause, and do no good to the Republican cause.'* The only special train to arrive on time for the meeting was the one from Gorey.

THE RALLY

The disruptions kept hundreds of people away and many townspeople, fearing trouble from the anti-Treaty side, stayed away. But despite the heavy rain, sleet and even thunder and lightning, a large determined throng assembled in St Peter's Square to hear Michael Collins speak. 'The Big Fella' and his colleagues arrived at 3pm to address the crowd, and were greeted by lots of cheering and shouts of 'Up Collins!' while the Redmondstown Band entertained the crowd outside Cousins' Mineral Water factory.

Originally O'Keeffe's Malthouse, Cousins was in business here until 1968 and today the building is occupied by Red Books independent bookshop. The square was a popular venue for political rallies when the area was a completely open space. St Peter's Church, which once stood in the centre of the square and just outside the town wall, was demolished subsequent to the sacking of the town by Cromwell in 1649 and the establishment of the new anti-Catholic regime. Peter's Gate (at the top of Peter's Street) was removed in the 1700s and the church ruins were cleared by the Corporation in the late 1800s.

The Anglo-Irish Treaty was signed in London on 6 December 1921 by Arthur Griffith, Michael Collins, Robert Barton, George Gavan Duffy and Éamonn Duggan and was ratified by Dáil Éireann on 7 January 1922. In the aftermath, however, Sinn Féin was split; Michael Collins with 64 others on

The old Cousins' Mineral Water plant on St Peter's Square, Wexford (now home to Red Books).
Michael Collins made his famous Wexford speech from the top of the steps seen left of centre.

| William Sears | J.J. Stafford | Richard Corish | Dr Vincent White |

the pro-Treaty side and Éamon de Valera and 56 members on the opposing anti-Treaty side.

Collins and the other dignitaries were led by the Mayor, Richard Corish. The foundries and other prominent businesses were represented on the platform and Kathleen Browne was among the political representatives who took their seats. The chairman, J.J. Stafford, opened the meeting and appealed to the crowd to set aside their differences. He pleaded with them to embrace the Treaty that Collins had signed just four months earlier that offered peace but divided the country into the Irish Free State and Northern Ireland. Next up was Sinn Féin TD, William Sears, proprietor and editor of the *Enniscorthy Echo*, followed by the Dublin TD, Professor Michael Hayes, Minister for Education, who also urged the people of Wexford to support the Treaty.

Michael Collins then ascended the steps of Cousins in the pouring rain to address the cheering crowd. With his charismatic personality he stirred up the throng with his fiery oratory and gestures. Of the Treaty he said *'Ireland would have control of all national activities. The Treaty was not perfect but they knew what it gave. The people should not surrender the bird in the hand for the charms, lent by distance, of the bird in the bush.'*

'Freedom is not a form of government,' he went on. *'Ireland suffered the greatest oppression of all under the republic of Cromwell. Was it not the presence of the British that deprived the nation of its liberty? And would their departure not restore liberty and give a chance of restoring Ireland's industries and its Gaelic life? Could not anybody understand that? Who could deny it?'*

'It is in our hands then to see that the remaining six counties also become free', he continued. *'That we are not completely free in all Ireland is largely due to the extent to which we are not a united people. We who made the Treaty were not responsible for that. It is the departure of the British troops that matters. It is this departure that makes us free from their interference. This departure is the one indispensable factor in our freedom.'*

'We are told the Treaty will not bring us peace. The Treaty has already brought us peace with our British enemy. If it will not bring us peace now, it will be because there are those who do not wish it to bring us peace. Is it by civil war, by shedding the blood of our brothers, that we can win peace and freedom? This is the language of treason, not of patriotism. Our existence is threatened now as no enemy from outside ever had the power to threaten it. There is grave danger of another long agony before our country, brought on by ourselves.'

'If we are plunged into a conflict between ourselves we should lose that sympathy which was so great an asset in our recent struggle. But if she [England] returns here as a result of our own strife, what world sympathy will we have then? And will not England be justified in her claim that she remained here only to govern us, because we were unable to do it ourselves?'

The *New Ross Standard* reported that next up to speak was the Mayor of Wexford, Richard Corish TD, who spoke about *'the general slump in trade and industrial life.'* He pointed to *'the present situation in Wexford, where practically two-thirds of the people were dependent on industrial success, and whose bread and butter depended on trade resumption.'* He said that *'although the Treaty was not an ideal one it was the best thing that could be got.'*

The Mayor was followed by Séamus Dwyer, TD for Dublin County and a personal friend of Michael Collins. Dwyer concluded his speech saying that *'the supporters of the Treaty would accept the will of the people on the issue and if the people decided against it, they of the Treaty would be found again where they were the last time – behind Collins, standing by the will of the people and maintaining it'*, which was followed by applause from the crowd. Séamus Dwyer was shot dead by an anti-Treaty IRA volunteer eight months later on 20 December as he stood in a shop in Rathmines.

Collins and his friend Harry Boland having a puck about before the Leinster Hurling Final between Dublin and Kilkenny in Croke Park, September 1921. They would both be shot dead the following summer, on opposing sides in the Civil War. (photo: Cork Examiner)

The final speaker was Dr Vincent White, TD, a medical practitioner and the then Mayor of Waterford. He had taken the seat occupied by William Archer Redmond, son of the Irish Parliamentary Party leader John Redmond, in the 1921 General Election. Also speaking in favour of the Treaty, Dr White said he believed that *'in the present stage of Irish affairs that the issue was a Free State or chaos. Today they were out fighting as plain men for the consummation of freedom and not for faction.'*

The meeting concluded and the now-sodden public cheered loudly and began to disperse. Shouts of 'Up Collins!' went up, mingled with some cries of 'Up the Republic!' and 'Up De Valera!' Michael Collins returned to Dublin on the special train that had been held up at Woodenbridge earlier in the day. It departed Wexford at 8pm with its passengers who had missed the rally and proceeded cautiously. At stations en route similar cheers went up for Collins with some too for De Valera.

GENERAL ELECTION

Under the provisions of the Anglo-Irish Treaty signed in 1921, a General Election was called for 16 June 1922. This Third Dáil was to be a provisional parliament that would pave the way for the formal establishment of the Irish Free State, a Dominion of the British Commonwealth. It would be known as the Free State Dáil from 1922 to 1937. Sinn Féin had won all seats, except the four in the University of Dublin, in the uncontested General Election of 1921. But the party was now divided between 65 pro-Treaty and 57 anti-Treaty candidates and this time there were other parties contesting the election. On 20 May 1922, Michael Collins (pro-Treaty) and Éamon de Valera (anti-Treaty) agreed to fight the election jointly to minimize losses for Sinn Féin. They also agreed that a sitting member would not be opposed by the other faction, which prevented voters in uncontested seats choosing between the pro- or anti-Treaty side.

The results of the General Election returned 58 seats for Sinn Féin (pro-Treaty), 36 for

Election poster for Sinn Féin's eight candidates in the 1922 general election in Collins' Cork constituency. (photo: Pathé)

Sinn Féin (anti-Treaty) and 34 seats went to other parties. The four Wexford seats went to: Richard Corish and Daniel O'Callaghan (Labour), Séamus Doyle (Sinn Féin, anti-Treaty) and Michael Doyle (Farmers' Party). In his Cork constituency, Michael Collins topped the poll with over thirty percent of the vote. De Valera was returned unopposed in Clare.

Although the pro-Treaty parties had secured support from over three-quarters of the electorate, the anti-Treaty forces sought the establishment of an All-Ireland Republic. The new Provisional Government appointed Michael Collins as Commander-in-Chief of the Free State Army. Just twelve days after the election, he ordered the bombardment of the Four Courts in Dublin, which was being occupied by a contingent of anti-Treaty IRA. This was the start of the Civil War.

The Free State army sent a group known as the 'Wexford Column' to Wexford on 8 July. They secured Gorey, followed by Enniscorthy after three days of fighting and finally reached Wexford, where they set up headquarters in the Talbot Hotel. County Wexford was one of the most violent counties during the Civil War, with killings and executions on both sides. The anti-Treaty faction continually attacked the county's railway network to disrupt the function of the Free State government and many 'big houses' went up in flames, in part against the Free State's political elite.

SHOOTING OF COLLINS

Arthur Griffith, who had negotiated the Treaty with Collins, died of natural causes on 12 August 1922. Ten days later, Michael Collins fell victim to the Civil War political assassinations. As head of the army, he travelled to his home county of Cork to inspect areas recently recovered from anti-Treaty forces, despite being strenuously advised against it. The county was regarded as an anti-Treaty IRA stronghold but Collins told his advisors *they won't shoot me in my own county.*

Collins' armed convoy left Portobello Barracks in Dublin on Sunday, 20 August and visited military installations along the way. Collins stayed at the military HQ in the Imperial Hotel in Cork City for two nights. He believed the Civil War would soon be over and had come south searching for peace. On Monday he visited his sister Mary and travelled to Cobh for a military review.

The last known photograph of Michael Collins alive (seated at the back of a yellow Leyland Eight Tourer, with Major General Emmet Dalton to his right), leaving Lee's Hotel in Bandon, County Cork before heading to Béal na mBláth. This remarkable picture was taken by then 18-year-old Agnes Hurley from Bandon on her Brownie box camera and discovered as part of her lost collection in an attic in Dublin in 2011.

Early on Tuesday morning the military detail carrying the Free State Commander-in-Chief drove from Cork City through Macroom, then headed south for Bandon. They were travelling through some of the most active anti-Treaty areas of south Cork and stopped at Long's public house in the little village of Béal na mBláth at about 8am to ask directions to Bandon. Collins briefly met in Lee's Hotel in Bandon with Major General Seán Hales, Officer-in-Command of the Free State forces in West Cork. They then continued on to Clonakilty, Roscarberry and Skibbereen.

The convoy left the Eldon Hotel in Skibbereen at 5pm and headed back to Cork. They detoured around Clonakilty on the way back because of a roadblock and stopped at the Four Alls Bar, owned by Collins' cousin Jeremiah, a few miles outside the town at Sam's Cross. There he told his older brother Seán: *'I'm going to settle this thing. I'm going to put an end to this bloody war'* and that he would *'go further with the British government once there is peace here. The British have given up their claim on us. When we begin to work together we can help those in the northeast.'* Having passed the remains of his childhood home in the nearby townland of Woodfield, burnt down by British troops the previous year, they arrived back in Lee's Hotel (now the Munster Arms) in time for tea.

Anti-Treaty forces had blocked all roads between Bandon and Cork City, forcing the convoy to return via Béal na mBláth. An ambush party numbering 25 to 30 lay in wait for hours until finally word came through that Collins' motorcade had left Bandon. They commandeered a cart, removed one of its wheels and blocked the road. It was shortly before darkness fell when the convoy came into sight.

In the ensuing thirty-minute firefight, Michael Collins was hit and lay dying face down on the road with a gaping hole at the base of his skull. It is believed that he was hit either by a ricochet or dum-dum bullet. His body was placed in the touring car and driven through the darkness to the Imperial Hotel in Cork. From there it was transferred to Shankiel Hospital for post-mortem. The next day, Collins' remains were transported onboard the *SS Classic* from Penrose Quay to Dublin.

Michael Collins was replaced as Commander-in-Chief of the Free State Army by Richard Mulcahy, husband of Wexford-born Min Ryan. He ordered the execution of anti-Treaty activists who were captured carrying firearms. This resulted in the shooting by firing squad of Wexford men James Parle, John Creane and Patrick Hogan outside the old Wexford Jail in March 1923. The Civil War continued until May 1923 and resulted in over 1,500 deaths.

The day after the shooting dead of Michael Collins. Free State soldiers and his sister Hannie examine the ambush site at Béal na mBláth, nine miles outside Bandon. (photo: Collins 22 Society)

Cultivating the tobacco crop in County Wexford

Outside the tobacco curing barn near Broadway in south Wexford in 1907. (photo: Keating collection)

AS FAR BACK as the early 1800s, tobacco was grown in the Wexford area. This followed legislation under the English monarchy that encouraged its production in this country. But when it threatened England's own tobacco industry and their trade with America, a new law was enacted in 1832 that halted the cultivation of the crop in Ireland. The act was repealed however in 1907 and production recommenced in County Wexford and elsewhere. Following the 1932 general election, the new Fianna Fáil government, in its protectionist policy and subsequent economic war with Britain, supported the industry in Ireland by reducing tobacco duty. It proved to be so profitable, however, with too many farmers becoming involved, the Minister for Agriculture, Dr Jim Ryan from Wexford, was obliged to reimpose controls. The industry finally collapsed with the outbreak of the Second World War.

Tobacco is said to have been first introduced into Europe from Virginia by the writer and explorer Sir Walter Raleigh in about 1586. Raleigh was granted 42,000 acres of land that included the town of Youghal in County Cork and Lismore in County Waterford by Elizabeth I – his reward for the part he played in suppressing the 16th century Desmond Rebellions. The queen herself gave smoking a try and soon the habit caught on among the population. Tobacco was placed under a duty of one percent in Elizabeth's reign.

When James I succeeded to the throne, declaring himself King of England and Ireland in 1603, he described smoking as a *'custome lothesome to the eye, hateful to the nose, harmful to the brain, dangerous to the lungs, and in the black and stinking fume thereof, nearest resembling the horrible stygian smoke of the pit that is bottomless'*. He levied an import tax of 35% on tobacco and the Catholic Church declared its use as sinful.

The cultivation of tobacco in England was prohibited under James I and this ban was extended to Ireland by Charles II in 1660. But despite the law, the historian and Jacobite sympathizer Thomas Carte in *The Improvement of Ireland* 1698, proposed the growing of the crop in this country: *'…a valuation should be given to the King: and so prohibit all forraign Tobacco: and in Lieu thereof sett up a Plantation here? The land is indifferently good for the same: the clymat warm enough: experience hath prov'd it: and further skill would make the tobacco sufficiently palatable.'* However, Carte's advice was not heeded by the relevant authorities.

Following America's Declaration of Independence in 1776, new legislation enacted in the 1790s under George III referred to taxation on imported tobacco and included the line: *'…encouragement should be given to such of the*

Advertisement in Tempest's Jubilee Annual in 1909.

produce and manufactures of Ireland as do not materially interfere with the commercial interests of Great Britain.' This was a concession to Ireland and its tenant farmers, who began cultivating tobacco, particularly in the eastern counties of the country.

By 1831, County Wexford, due in part to its favourable climate, reported extensive growing of tobacco. In Joseph McSweeny's *Essay on the Climate of Ireland*, published in 1830, he noted: *'[In] about 1632, artichokes, colly flowers, pompions and hops seem to have been first introduced and grow very well…if they had been introduced at an earlier period, there is little doubt but that they would have succeeded as well. The same reasoning holds good for the tobacco, cultivated at present to such an extent in the county of Wexford.'*

Despite objections from Daniel O'Connell and

the Limerick politician and future Chancellor of the Exchequer, Thomas Spring Rice, the Tobacco (Ireland) Act was passed in Westminster in 1832, prohibiting the sale, manufacture and consumption of tobacco grown in Ireland. This again halted the cultivation of the crop in this country. But supported by the MP for Wexford, William Redmond and Arthur Griffith, the then editor of the *United Irishman* newspaper, the development of the tobacco crop was again promoted in 1898 by Colonel Nugent Everard of Randalstown, County Meath. Everard was granted a special government licence to experiment in the growing of 'legalized seeds'. From Joyce's *Ulysses*, set in Dublin in 1904: *'You could grow any mortal thing in Irish soil…and there was that colonel Everard down there in Navan growing tobacco…Col. N.T. Everard was a gentleman farmer who in 1904 was conducting what he regarded as a successful twenty-acre experiment in tobacco growing.'*

Between 1904 and 1913, twenty-seven people held licences to grow tobacco in seven counties in Ireland. Tobacco cultivation was very labour intensive however, requiring 700 hours per acre – twice that for potatoes. In County Limerick, Lord Dunraven was one who experimented in growing tobacco. He set up the Adare Cigarette Company on his estate and employed about seventy people who graded the leaves into different categories of quality. However, the factory was destroyed in a fire in 1917 and never re-opened.

Tobacco workers at Randalstown near Navan in 1914. (photo: Meath County Library)

Tobacco grower, from the Franciscan Capuchin Annual, 1933. It was printed by John English & Co., Wexford from 1934-57).

William Sears, Sinn Féin TD and proprietor of the *Enniscorthy Echo*, proposed in the Dáil in 1926 the establishment of a special committee to consider the question of the remission of excise duty on tobacco grown in the Free State. Following the decisive victory of Fianna Fáil in the general election of 1932, the new Taoiseach, Éamon de Valera, immediately implemented the recommendation.

The party's stated goal was self-sufficiency in agricultural produce and this included their support for the tobacco industry by way of the removal of duty on growing the crop. The new government embarked on a protectionist policy and tariffs were introduced on a wide range of imported goods, mainly from Britain. This resulted in the Anglo-Irish Trade War of 1932-38. At the Fianna Fáil Ard Fheis in 1933, the Minister for Agriculture, Wexford TD, Dr Jim Ryan, promised 10,000 acres under tobacco and that cigarettes were to contain a percentage of native tobacco.

By 1934 about 750 acres were dedicated to cultivating tobacco, mainly in County Wexford, but also in counties Carlow, Kilkenny, Meath, Kildare, Laois, Offaly and Wicklow. It was proving to be a very profitable crop for the growers. But the government soon realized that with fewer taxes being collected on imported tobacco, they had to move to restrict the acreage under tobacco. Under Minister Ryan's new Tobacco Act, 1934, a maximum of two acres could be grown by an individual. Cultivation was also now restricted to those who had grown tobacco under licence the previous year. Only the lower-yielding variety *Orinoco* was now permitted to be planted.

Dr Jim Ryan, Wexford TD and Minister for Agriculture, 1932-47.

With the onset of the Second World War, cattle prices in Ireland collapsed. Farmers were desperate; some turned their hand at growing tobacco but many failed to grasp its complexities. The crop was often poorly grown and harvested. The experiment in tobacco self-sufficiency in Ireland had ended. *Béaloideas*, the Journal of the Folklore of Ireland

Tobacco harvest time on the Keating farm at Yoletown near Tacumshane in 1907. (photo: Keating collection)

Society, featured an article concerning the effect on the failure of tobacco growing in Wexford: '...*it was recorded that in the Clonroche district of County Wexford people smoked the dry withered bark near the stump of a furze bush as a substitute for tobacco.*'

BARONY OF FORTH

With encouragement from Canon Luke Doyle, William Redmond MP and Sir Horace Plunkett, pioneer of the farmers' co-operatives, a meeting of the Forth Farmers' Association was held in Tagoat in 1903. It was proposed that tobacco cultivation be instigated on an experimental basis in the area. Twelve farmers were to set aside one acre each to grow the crop, with the backing of the Department of Agriculture. The Forth Tobacco Growers Association was formed and a 'curing' barn, one of many at the time, was erected in about 1907 between Tagoat and Broadway.

Tobacco was cultivated at the Keating farm in Yoletown, Tacumshane, a couple of miles from Broadway, between 1908 and 1913 in what became known as 'the tobacco field'. After a break of twenty years, Patrick Keating again grew tobacco from 1933 to 1941. Both *Burley*, a heavy and high-yielding tobacco suitable for pipe-smoking, and *Orinoco*, a lighter cigarette tobacco, were propagated. Requiring rich soil, manure was spread on the field in early December and ploughed in immediately. When spring arrived, the seeds had to be sown in timber-framed hotbeds filled with horse manure to germinate.

The beds were protected by sheets of glass. In May, the field was required to be re-ploughed before harrowing and planting. The seedlings were carefully pricked out and soon ready to be transplanted to the field. Many however were also sold locally.

Planting *Jerusalem artichokes*, a species of sunflower, helped to protect the seedlings from wind damage. The tobacco plants usually grew to about three feet in height. In June, weeding was necessary and this was carried out using a small horse or pony pulling a grubber. Some weeding had to be done by hand and this was back-breaking work. Side shoots known as suckers as well as the flower buds had to be removed from each plant to increase yield. Harvesting began in August and cutting was done using a billhook. The leaves were then stored in a shed on the farm.

The plants were tied in bunches of five, hung on canes and transported on a cart fitted with a timber frame to the curing barn in Broadway, where growers were required to supply their own labour – three women for each acre of tobacco grown. The next stage consisted of grading the tobacco and tying the leaves into bunches. In its raw, freshly picked state, the green tobacco leaf was too wet to ignite and needed to be smoked by 'curing'. The Broadway shed used steam to dry the leaves. But when the steam engine broke down it

Patrick Keating (centre) of Yoletown Farm taking a load of tobacco leaves to the curing barn in Broadway, August 1933. (photo: Keating collection)

was found to be too expensive to repair and so coke fires were used instead. When the leaves were dry, ten or twelve were tied together with thread. Known as a 'hand' of tobacco, these were stored in barrels or sacking, awaiting collection by the Imperial Tobacco Company.

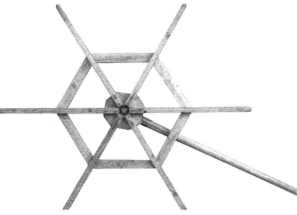

Measuring implement made by Patrick Keating, used to mark equal intervals in drills before sowing tobacco seedlings on his farm in Tacumshane.

Patrick Keating meticulously recorded all farm activity in his diaries. Encouraged by the new government policy of self-sufficiency and the removal of duty on tobacco-growing, he began preparing his first hotbeds in March 1933. In that first season Patrick had propagated 8,700 tobacco plants for his own use and sold 8,800 locally. From his one-and-a-half acres dedicated to tobacco growing, he sent a further 3,500 out of the county by rail to as far away as Galway and Sligo. Yields were less in subsequent years, however, as a result of the government ban on planting *Burley* tobacco. The high profits made in 1933 were never repeated and this resulted in a reduction in the number of growers in the country.

NORTH WEXFORD

Mount St Benedict school near Gorey was the unlikely location for a tobacco factory in the north of the county. The establishment was run by a Benedictine priest, Father Dominic Sweetman. He was born John Sweetman into a prosperous landowning family in Clohamon near Bunclody in 1872. He entered Downside Abbey, a Benedictine monastery in Somerset, in 1891 and was ordained there in 1899. He volunteered for a year as a chaplain to the British forces in the Boer War in South Africa (1899-1902) before taking up a teaching post back in Downside for a number of years.

BALLYOWEN CHEROOTS

ORDER DIRECT FROM

BALLYOWEN FACTORY

GOREY, CO. WEXFORD

AND THUS SAVE 50 %

Price **2d.** Each (over 4 ins. long)

FREE SAMPLES SENT to any address on receipt of post card

Advert from 1920 for 'Ballyowen' cheroots (a cigar with both ends open), manufactured at Mount St Benedict.

Father Dominic Sweetman with workers in his tobacco factory in Mount St Benedict school at Hollyfort near Gorey, 1920s. (photo: Joseph Cashman)

Sweetman returned to Ireland and established a Benedictine school at Ballinapierce outside Enniscorthy in 1905 and was joined there by three other monks from Downside. But this soon proved to be too small to cater for the number of boys who wanted to enrol and he needed to find a larger building. In 1907, Mount Nebo, a country mansion in Hollyfort close to Gorey, was purchased by another John Sweetman, former politician and cousin of Father Dominic, who had also been educated at Downside. The house became the new school and was renamed Mount St Benedict in 1909.

The school, with no more than fifty pupils at its peak, attracted some notable boys such as the future politicians Seán MacBride and James Dillon. Father Sweetman turned republican after the 1916 Rising and was accused of harbouring Sinn Féiners in 'The Mount', as it was known locally, during the War of Independence. A colourful character by all accounts, he claimed to have studied the growing of tobacco during his time in South Africa. He cultivated the crop on the grounds of the school and set up his own tobacco factory. The leaves were used to make cigars, cigarettes and pipe tobacco under the brand name 'Ballyowen'. The factory employed up to ten local women and sometimes boys from the school worked as volunteers. Eventually, Sweetman was forced to close when he fell foul of customs and excise, and the school itself closed in about 1925.

Augustus Welby Pugin – 'God's architect' in Wexford

St. Aidan's Cathedral, Enniscorthy, Augustus Pugin's largest church building in Ireland. (photo: Des Kiely)

AUGUSTUS PUGIN, in his short life span of only 40 years, was a leading figure in the 19th century Gothic Revival that drew its inspiration from European medieval architecture. He was born in London in 1812, the son of Auguste-Charles Pugin, a French immigrant architectural draughtsman, and Catherine Welby. Augustus learned drawing from his father, who was a promoter of the neo-Gothic style.

Most of the Houses of Parliament in London were destroyed in a fire in 1834 and a new Westminster Palace, with the addition of the Big Ben clock tower, was designed by Sir Charles Barry. The external and internal neo-Gothic ornamental decoration was designed by Augustus Pugin and the new building was completed in 1860.

Having converted to Catholicism in 1835, Augustus Pugin made the acquaintance of John Talbot, Earl of Shrewsbury and of Waterford, of Alton Towers in Staffordshire. Talbot, himself a Catholic, became a noted patron of Pugin, commissioning him to build churches throughout England. Talbot's wife Maria was a daughter of William Talbot of Castle Talbot, Blackwater,

Augustus Welby Pugin (1812-1852).

County Wexford. Her uncle, John Hyacinth Talbot of Ballytrent House, was an MP for New Ross, who had married firstly into the powerful political Redmond family and secondly the Power Whiskey family, having married Elizabeth, sister of Sir James Power of Edermine House.

A meeting between Augustus Pugin and John Hyacinth Talbot at Alton Towers in 1839 led to commissions in Ireland for the much sought-after architect. Pugin visited Ireland about ten times between then and his early death in 1852. Most of his assignments were in County Wexford through the patronage of Talbot. Regarded as his best buildings in Ireland are the cathedrals of St. Mary's in Killarney and his largest church in Ireland: St. Aidan's in Enniscorthy. Construction began in Killarney in 1842 and the following year in Enniscorthy. But the building of both churches was interrupted by lack of funds during the Great Famine of 1845-9.

St. Aidan's Cathedral, Enniscorthy c.1900 with the colourful ornate stencilling that Pugin used, imitating the medieval churches of Europe. (photo: Robert French/NLI)

St. Aidan's Cathedral was built to replace an older church on the site, which was erected in 1809. When the nave was completed in 1849 the old building, around which the new cathedral was built, was demolished. On the death of Pugin, Dublin architect James Joseph McCarthy was engaged to complete the interior following Pugin's designs. McCarthy was a follower of Pugin and the Gothic Revival. The high altar, added in 1857, was provided by the sculptor James Pearse, father of Pádraig and William Pearse, who were both executed for their part in the Easter Rising of 1916. When the spire and central tower were added in 1871, however, they began to collapse and had to be taken down and rebuilt.

Edermine chapel, built for Sir James and Lady Jane Power. (photo: Des Kiely)

Pugin's decorative stencilled patterns on the interior of the cathedral were overpainted in white in 1970 but these were restored as part of a £1million restoration in 1994. The restorers consulted Pugin's chapel at Edermine House, where the roof and wall decoration is preserved in their original state.

Sir James Power, who married John Hyacinth Talbot's daughter Jane in 1843, met Augustus Pugin on a visit to Ballytrent. The Power Whiskey family were benefactors of St. Aidan's and Pugin was commissioned to design a chapel next to Edermine House on the Power estate, south of Enniscorthy. It was built in 1860-2, after Pugin's death, and probably supervised either by his son Edward or J.J. McCarthy. The design and plan are similar to those used for the private chapel for the Cliffe family at Bellevue House on the far side of the River Slaney in Ballyhogue.

Bellevue was originally the residence of George Ogle, who was an MP for Wexford. In 1798 he was commander of his own infantry in the Shelmalier volunteer yeomanry, 'Ogle's Royal Blues', that earned the name 'Ogle's Bloody Blues'. In 1825 the estate was purchased by Anthony Cliffe, who improved and extended the mansion as well as building

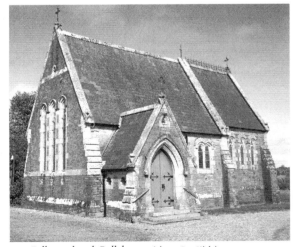

Bellevue chapel, Ballyhogue. (photo: Des Kiely)

houses on the estate for the workers and their families and so creating the village of Ballyhogue. The landed gentry family, who converted to Catholicism, had this private chapel built adjoining the house. Although it has been attributed to A.W. Pugin, it may have been designed by J.J. McCarthy in the Pugin style. The Cliffes were very popular in the area but at the outbreak of the Civil War in 1922 they moved to safety in England. In January 1923 the house was burnt to the ground in an anti-Treaty IRA attack. The little chapel survived, however, and between 1947 and 1952 served as both a national school and church for parishioners of Ballyhogue. The building was restored and rededicated in 1965.

Colonel Henry Alcock of Wilton Castle was a brother of William, who was famously shot dead by his election opponent John Colclough of Tintern Abbey in a duel in 1807. He subsequently inherited the family seat in 1813, following William's death. Henry donated an acre of land rent free for the building of a church in the nearby village of Bree in 1837. The construction of the Church of the Assumption was completed two years later to a design by A.W. Pugin and commissioned by John Hyacinth Talbot. This would make it Pugin's first church building in Ireland. It follows his later designs for St. James's Church in Ramsgrange and St. Peter's College chapel in Wexford.

St. Mary's Church in Tagoat has been described as an example of Pugin's best work on a small church. In Thomas Lacy's *Sights and Scenes in Our*

Church of the Assumption in Bree, probably Pugin's first church in Ireland. (photo: Des Kiely)

Fatherland (1863), he called it '...one of the most perfect and regular ecclesiastical edifices to be seen in any of the rural parishes in the diocese of Ferns.'

St. Mary's was yet another church commissioned by John Hyacinth Talbot, who lived just four miles away in Ballytrent House. Talbot had it erected in

St. Mary's Church, Tagoat, regarded by many as one of Pugin's most important parish churches in Ireland. (photo: Des Kiely)

1843 in memory of his first wife Ann Eliza Redmond, from whom he inherited the Redmond estate, including Ballytrent. She was 19 years old when they married in 1822 but died four years later. The first Mass to be celebrated in St. Mary's was in 1846 for the funeral of its own parish priest, Canon Walter Rowe, who had supervised its construction.

Work on St. Alphonsus' Church in Barntown commenced in 1844 and was completed in 1848, using four different types of stone quarried locally. It was modelled on the quaint 13th century thatched church of St. Michael in Longstanton, Cambridgeshire. With its unusual double bellcote, the village church has also been imitated near Philadelphia, in South Dakota and elsewhere. It was named after the Neapolitan theologian Alphonsus Liguori, founder of the Redemptorists and the patron saint of confessors. In Phoebe Stanton's 1972 biography of Pugin she says that in his churches at Barntown, Tagoat and Gorey the 'emphasis on materials, the excellence of

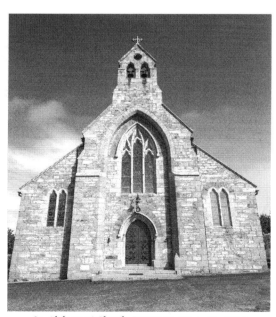

St. Alphonsus' Church, Barntown. (photo: Des Kiely)

St. Peter's College chapel, Summerhill, Wexford town, c.1900. (photo: Robert French/NLI)

the workmanship, the lack of ornament, the dignified and heavy proportions are more than their characteristics – they are their graces.'

A.W. Pugin laid the foundation stone for the chapel at St. Peter's College overlooking Wexford town in 1838 and the first Mass was celebrated two years later. A former seminary and now an all-male secondary school, the college was founded in 1819. A large house dating from c.1790 was purchased the previous year and extended over many years, creating the college complex. The chapel, one of Pugin's first great works in Ireland, which is still used for school ceremonies, has a magnificent stained-glass rose window by John Hardman of Birmingham that features the coat of arms of the Talbot family. The two chapel bells were cast by Thomas Mears at his Whitechapel Bell Foundry in London and shipped to Wexford for installation.

St. James's Church, Ramsgrange. (photo: Des Kiely)

Construction of the Church of St. James in Ramsgrange began in 1838. The village was at the time part of the united parish of St. James and Hook. It has been argued that the design of the church did not come from Augustus Pugin. But this was shown to be the case not only by documentary evidence but also by the Pugin Society, who point to internal evidence of the building's fabric and sophisticated details that the designer had to be Pugin. Its exposed timber roof construction bears close similarities to Pugin's chapel at St. Peter's College. In 1841, the *Catholic Directory and Annual Register* referred to the church as 'a very large and beautiful Church according to a plan furnished by Mr Pugin'. The building took five years to complete and the tower, erected following Pugin's original drawings, was added in 1870. The tower was to have been finished with a steeple but instead was given a flat capping with under-scale spikes at the corners, untypical of the Pugin style.

Sir Thomas Esmonde of Ballynastragh House near Gorey was one of only a small number of Catholic gentry living in Ireland at the time. He donated land on the outskirts of Gorey for the construction of a new church to replace the old thatched chapel at Gorey Bridge. Pugin submitted his designs for the new St. Michael's Church in 1839. Wexford architect Richard Pierce oversaw the construction while already at work on St. Peter's College chapel in Wexford. Pugin on this occasion adopted Romanesque round-arched style windows and doorways, typical only of some of this early work. The cruciform-

Construction of St. Michael's Church, Gorey, was overseen by Richard Pierce and completed in 1843. (photo: NLI)

shaped building features a crossing tower capped with stepped battlements and a European-style turret with conical roof.

Augustus Welby Pugin had a very short working life, from 1835 until his death in 1852. But in these seventeen years he designed more than a hundred buildings in Britain, Ireland and Australia, including the elaborate decorative finishes for the Houses of Parliament in London which he worked on for eight years. Pugin wrote eight influential books on Gothic architecture. He also had to suffer the death of two of his three wives. He was putting himself under such stress that in 1852, while travelling by train from his home in Ramsgate to London with his eldest son, 17-year-old Edward from his second wife, Pugin suffered a complete physical and mental breakdown. He died a number of months later. The writer and historian Rosemary Hill, in her 2007 Pugin biography *God's Architect*, places his work as an artist alongside his changing religious beliefs, the bitterness of his last years and his deteriorating medical condition.

After his death, Pugin's son Edward continued his father's successful architectural practice with various partners. Together with his brother-in-law and former pupil, the Cork-born architect George Ashlin, he designed the churches at Our Lady's Island in the south of the county and Kilanerin, north of Gorey, at the other end. Also with Ashlin, he built the spectacular cathedral of St. Colman in Cobh. Unlike his father, Edward designed churches with open sight lines to the altar and seldom with rood screens that separated the main body from the altar. He also collaborated with the architects Richard Pierce and J.J. McCarthy.

RICHARD PIERCE'S TWIN CHURCHES
The Franciscans came to Wexford in about 1255. The friary was suppressed in 1540 as part of the Dissolution of the Monasteries under Henry VIII. A new community arrived in 1615 and, despite the killing of seven friars by Cromwellian soldiers in 1649, they later recovered their friary and restored their church in 1690. But under William III, the friars were banished from Ireland in 1698. The first Relief Act, also known as the 'Papists Act', was passed in 1778 and the Penal Laws were ultimately rescinded by the 1829 Roman Catholic Relief Act, finally delivering Catholic Emancipation.

The present Franciscan Friary was built in 1802. The church also served as the parish church and, due to an expanding congregation, was extended in 1812 and again in 1827 and the four-storey bell tower was added in the 1850s. At a public meeting in the friary in January 1850 it was proposed to build two new churches, one at either end of the town. Rev. James Roche, born in Duncormick in 1801 and parish priest of Ferns, was transferred to Wexford in June 1850. His younger brother John was a member of the Franciscan friars. Bishop Myles Murphy, a former parish priest of Wexford, stated that both churches should be identical to avoid

Rowe Street Church, Wexford, one of the twin churches designed by Richard Pierce.

'jealousy and unpleasant comparisons amongst the townspeople.'

The sites for the two churches lay just outside the old town wall. The church for the north end (Immaculate Conception) was to be located at the junction of John Street and Rowe Street, close to the Franciscan friary. Its twin church on the south end (Assumption) was to be built between Bride Street and King Street, on the site of a Quaker graveyard and the old medieval church of St. Bride, destroyed on the order of Oliver Cromwell in 1649. Funding for the twin churches had already begun under Bishop Murphy with subscriptions collected in each district. Contributions were also made by many wealthy people in the town as well as Wexford emigrants around the world.

Richard Pierce was appointed in 1851 as the architect to design both churches in the Gothic Revival style, made popular by Augustus Pugin. He had acted as overseer of Pugin's churches in Enniscorthy, Gorey, Killarney and an extension to Maynooth College. He was an older brother of the ironmaster James Pierce and now had his own architectural practice. Richard is believed to have been born in the parish of Kilmore c.1801. He married Ann Kelly of Wexford town in 1833 and the family lived in a large house in the townland of Tenacre near Tomhaggard. The contractor for the building of the twin churches was Thomas Willis, who was himself the architect of other Wexford churches, including the Presbyterian Church on Anne Street and St. Ibar's in Castlebridge. Both twin churches were constructed from pink sandstone quarried at Park in the north of the town and finished in Wicklow granite.

Richard Pierce died aged 53 in 1854, two years after his mentor, Pugin, and four years before the completion of the two churches. His son, also Richard, continued some of the work but J.J. McCarthy, another follower of Pugin's neo-Gothic style, was commissioned to complete the buildings following Pierce's specifications. The first Masses were celebrated in both churches by Canon Roche a week apart in April 1858.

Bride Street Church, Wexford, before the surrounding wall and railings were added. (photo: NLI)

The magnificent Harry Clarke window in Bride Street Church. (photo: Des Kiely)

Thomas Earley, who had worked for Pugin with Hardman of Birmingham, was involved in the interior decoration and stained-glass windows. All the decorative work was completed by 1881. The ornamental perimeter railings were supplied by James Pierce from his nearby Folly Mills Iron Works (later Pierce's Foundry). In 1918, a stained-glass window for Bride Street Church was commissioned by Mrs Matilda O'Keefe of Faythe House to commemorate her son William, who was killed in France in WWI. Designed in the Art Nouveau style by Harry Clarke, it is one of only two of his works in the county – the other being the Lea-Wilson window in Christ Church, Gorey.

The 1918-19 flu pandemic caused over 500 deaths in Wexford

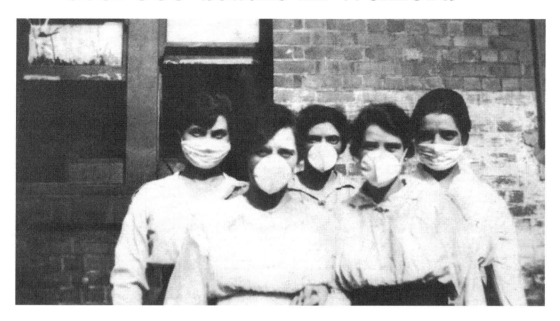

THE INFLUENZA pandemic that moved across Ireland for eight months, from June 1918 to February 1919, infected one-fifth of the population and killed over 23,000. Worldwide, deaths were estimated at 20 million and possibly many millions more. It mainly affected those aged 25-35 and under 5. In Ireland, the flu was responsible for more deaths than the Easter Rising, the War of Independence and the Civil War combined. By mid-July the threat had receded, only for the infection to reappear in an even more lethal second wave in October. It is estimated that some 22,000 people in County Wexford were infected and a total of 566 deaths in the county were certified as having been caused primarily by the outbreak.

People in Ireland were preoccupied at the time with the war in Europe that was to end in November 1918. Over 850 people from Wexford died in the First World War. John Redmond's Home Rule Act of 1914 was put on hold until after the conflict. Redmond's own brother Willie, who had been MP for East Clare since 1892, was killed in action in Flanders in June 1917. His vacant seat was won by Éamon de Valera. John Redmond, leader of the Irish Parliamentary Party, died in London on 6 March 1918. His remains were returned to Wexford and interred in the family vault in St. John's Graveyard on John Street.

'Mysterious scourge is spreading', ran the headline in the *Irish Independent* on 20 June 1918, reporting on a *'virulently infectious disease resembling influenza'* spreading throughout Belfast. Troops sailing home from the battlefields brought the flu into Ireland. The plague reached Dublin the next day but this first wave proved to be relatively mild. The newspapers reverted to coverage of the war in Europe as the German Army launched an offensive along the River Marne in France, in what would prove to be its last in the conflict.

Throughout WWI, censorship was imposed on all news emanating from the war zones of Europe. First reports from the United States, France, Germany and Britain of deaths from a new deadly influenza were suppressed in order to maintain morale. Spain had remained neutral and newspapers were therefore free to report when King Alfonso XIII, the Prime Minister, several government ministers as well as thousands of people in Madrid fell gravely ill with the flu. Stories emerged of the outbreak of the epidemic in Spain but not elsewhere, resulting in it being dubbed the 'Spanish flu'. The Japanese called it 'American influenza', while to Irish and British troops it was known as 'Flanders grippe [flu]'. It was not until 1933 that it was identified as the H1N1A virus.

In mid-October 1918, the flu re-appeared and this second wave would prove to be a lot more lethal than the first. Dublin, Kildare and Belfast were hit hardest, with deaths trebling. Schools and public buildings were forced to close. By the third week of October, the disease had reached Gorey. The Tara Hill area was particularly affected and the workhouse infirmary was reported to have received 200 patients, including some of its own nursing staff. New Ross was even harder hit, with 950 cases reported and 38 deaths by the beginning of November. Schools and some shops in the town were shut.

Enniscorthy Cathedral cancelled its annual retreat for fear of spreading the virus and much of the town was sprayed with disinfectant. *The People* newspaper reported that *'Every second person one meets reeks of eucalyptus, while in the schools and buildings disinfectants are liberally used. Everything that medical science could suggest is being done with the view of minimising the effects of the disease'*. All schools were closed, with many children reportedly falling ill. In the second week of November, twelve people died with the disease and over 300 people in the town and surrounding areas were reported to have caught the virus. This was a relatively low death rate compared to other districts. The district medical officer, Dr Thomas Kelly, advised against the holding of wakes or returning the bodies of those Enniscorthy people who died elsewhere. Dr Kelly requested the appointment of a second doctor and the vacancy was filled by Dr John Pierse, eldest son of Dr Thomas Pierse, Wexford town's medical officer. However, by the third week John, followed by his wife and child, had themselves succumbed to the disease.

Newtownbarry (Bunclody) and surrounding areas were also badly hit. The *Enniscorthy Guardian* reported one heartbreaking case of a family that lost three young children on the same day and while their bodies were being removed, the mother, father and the rest of the family had to be taken to hospital. The workhouse in Enniscorthy was forced to move some of their beds to the fever hospital in order to accommodate families from Newtownbarry. Travelling by train was believed by some to place people at risk of catching the flu. There were many reports of the continual sound of church bells ringing for the unprecedented number of funerals.

Unrelated, on 10 October 1918, the mailboat RMS *Leinster* left Kingstown (Dún Laoghaire) for Holyhead with some 771 people, including about 500 servicemen returning from leave. It was torpedoed twice by the German submarine *UB-123*. The sinking resulted in the death of 569: the greatest ever loss of life in the Irish Sea and the highest ever death toll on an Irish-owned ship. James Carraher from Wexford town was the boatswain, in charge of equipment and the crew. He was remembered for safely moving many passengers, including a baby, onto a raft and waiting with them for hours to be rescued. Germany had approached US President Wilson to end the war just four days earlier, but the sinking is believed to have prolonged the conflict, such as it angered the Allies.

Unscrupulous companies exploited

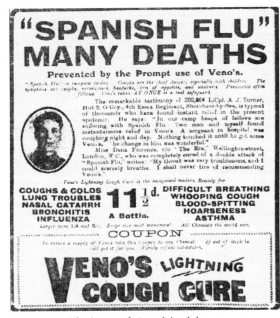

Veno's Lightning Cough Cure claimed that Lance Corporal Turner "found instantaneous relief" and Miss Dena Florence was "completely cured of a double attack of Spanish flu".

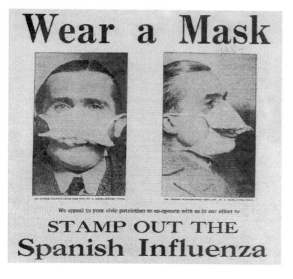

Wear a Mask

We appeal to your civic patriotism to co-operate with us in our effort to

STAMP OUT THE
Spanish Influenza

people's fears due to a lack of scientific knowledge on how to prevent the spread of the virus. 'You cannot catch influenza if you use Milton', read an advertisement for their mouthwash. Gallaher's High Toast snuff claimed it would 'prevent influenza'.

Dr Williams' Pink Pills for Pale People promised 'a miraculous cure'. Whiskey and hot water was the most effective remedy on offer to ease symptoms and was administered in most institutions, including the workhouses.

The Irish Times ran with the stark headline: *'Influenza epidemic in Ireland – Heavy death toll; Efforts to combat the disease.'* In Dublin, Glasnevin Cemetery was overwhelmed with the continued succession of funeral processions towards the end of October.

The Spanish flu was reported to be spreading rapidly in Wexford town in early November. All schools were closed and disinfected. According to *The People*, 200 cases were reported to the Wexford Board of Guardians by Dr Thomas Pierse, the town's medical officer. But soon he was reporting about 1,000 cases – almost one in twelve of the town's population. He too advised against holding wakes, which he believed were spreading the infection. On 16 November, *The People* reported: *'Many persons have been confined to bed with the malady, which appears to be coming more severe. Delirium, feverishness, headache, stomach troubles and general pains have characterised it. Then in a few instances people have succumbed after a few hours' illness, and their bodies have become discoloured and have had to be coffined. Nothing has happened in this country so general and so severe for generations; there must be more than fifteen hundred cases down in Wexford at present. A regular panic has been caused by the deaths which have occurred after a few hours illness. When the malady attacks the chest it becomes very serious. The sudden seizures are also very serious and a doctor should always be consulted. We have reason to fear recurrence of the epidemic from time to time. A plague of some kind follows all great wars.'*

Several prominent members of the Wexford senior hurling team were down with the flu, forcing the All-Ireland Final against Limerick to be deferred

The Wexford team that won the delayed 1918 All-Ireland Football Final against Tipperary, making it four in a row. The match was played in February 1919. (photo: GAA)

until 26 January 1919. Limerick won the championship, beating Wexford 9-5 to 1-3 in the final. The Leinster Football Final had also been deferred and took place on 19 January 1919, when Wexford beat Louth. The All-Ireland Football Final took place on 16 February, with Wexford beating Tipperary. Wexford had now won an unprecedented four-in-a-row All-Ireland titles, having also won in the three previous years against Kerry, Mayo and Clare. Tipperary's top point-scorer, Davy Tobin, missed the game due to the flu. Wexford county handball champion Dan Farrell died a few weeks after apparently having recovered from the virus.

When the truce was signed between Germany and the Allies on 11 November 1918, at 'the eleventh hour of the eleventh day of the eleventh month', ending the First World War, bonfires were lit in Enniscorthy to celebrate the armistice, despite the epidemic, though in other parts of the county the public mood was much more muted.

In the general election of December 1918, Sinn Féin won a landslide victory, defeating the Irish Parliamentary Party and winning 73 of the 105 seats. Roger Sweetman, a barrister, was returned for Wexford North and Dr Jim Ryan, who had a practice in Wexford town, was elected for Wexford South. All winning candidates refused to take their seats in the British House of Commons. Instead, they founded a separate parliament – Dáil Éireann – on 21 January 1919 and declared independence from Britain, thus precipitating the War of Independence.

The total number of deaths recorded in 1918 in County Wexford attributed to the Spanish flu was 348. The county had the third highest mortality rate in Leinster, after Kildare and Dublin. In mid-February 1919 a third wave hit Wexford but was less severe. It accounted for another 218 deaths where influenza was certified as the primary cause. It was the west and southwest of the country, where the first and second waves were less harsh, that would suffer the most deaths in 1919, with the third wave peaking in March and April.

People become immune to an influenza virus after catching it. However, viruses are constantly changing and the Influenza A virus can sometimes go through an abrupt 'antigenic shift', resulting in a new deadly strain. The global flu epidemic of 1918 has been described as 'the greatest medical holocaust in history'. It may have killed as many as the Black Death of 1345-53, which resulted in the deaths of up to 75 to 200 million. An influenza vaccine was not available in 1918; the first was not created until the 1950s. Since 1918, pandemics have occurred on four occasions. In 1957, the Asian flu was responsible for between 1 and 4 million deaths. The Hong Kong flu of 1968 killed about one million. In 2009, over a quarter of a million people worldwide died of the H1N1 flu. The first known cases of Covid-19 emerged in Wuhan, China in 2019 and quickly spread worldwide.

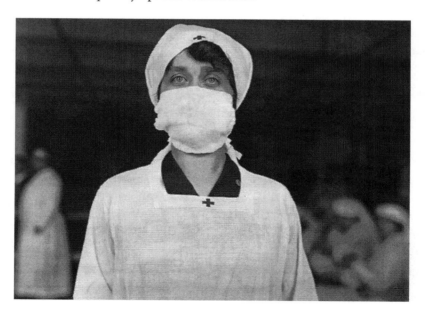

Shot dead by aunt who feared eviction in Killinick

*'The Sanctuary' is one of the oldest inhabited thatched houses in Ireland, dating back to 1610.
It was originally the rectory to Killinick Church. (photo: Dawn Ward)*

JANE O'BRIEN (née Cousins) lived just outside the village of Killinick, County Wexford, in the house of her brother William Cousins. Following the death of William in 1931, his son John told his aunt that she would soon have to move out of the farmhouse to make way for his new bride, to whom he was now engaged. Sixty-year-old Jane shot her nephew John dead using his own shotgun on Easter Saturday night in 1932. She was subsequently found guilty of murder but received a reprieve on account of her age and gender.

Sanctuary is a townland outside the village of Killinick on the road to Tacumshane and gets its name from 'The Sanctuary' – one of the oldest inhabited thatched houses in Ireland. The dwelling dates back to 1610 and was originally the rectory to Killinick Church. It is located behind the present-day St Enoch's Church of Ireland, built in 1828 on the site of an older church. But one who was not afforded sanctuary was the unfortunate John Cousins, who died from gunshot wounds inflicted by his aunt.

William Cousins married Kathleen Ennis in 1897 and they had just one child, John, who was born the following year. Kathleen died in 1920, aged about 55, and William continued to work his five-acre farm and live in their substantial farmhouse called 'The Sanctuary'.

William's sister, Jane, lived in a cottage two miles away in Yoletown. She was married to Andrew O'Brien and they too had one child, also named John. Andrew worked for the railway and was based at Rosslare Harbour. He moved without her to work in Scotland and later to London. William asked Jane to move in with him in Sanctuary following the death of his wife, as he had lots of room in the house for them both and their two boys and she could help with the household chores. Jane agreed to this arrangement in 1920.

William died in December 1931, aged about 64, without leaving a will. This meant that his estate would automatically pass to his 33-year-old son John, who was employed locally as a farm labourer. Jane was concerned about what the future would now hold for herself and her own son. It was shortly after the death of his father that John announced that he was engaged to Annie (Nan) Maguire, a neighbour ten years his junior, whom he had known all her life, and that it would soon be time for Jane and her son to leave the house. He said they planned to marry the following December.

But Jane would later claim in a statement: "Before I came to Sanctuary I discussed with John as follows – *'Now John, in years to come you might be getting married, and I could go to the road'* and that John replied: *'As long as you stay I'll never think of a woman, and never marry'* and that he would never forget my son John." From the time they announced their engagement, a series of unsigned postcards began to arrive at the home of Nan Maguire as well as John Cousins' home. They accused Nan of seeing other men and both Nan and John assumed they were coming from Jane. Nan later claimed that Jane confronted her on the road one day as she was walking with John. Jane said to her that "the place is John's and you have nothing to do with it."

John Cousins was an active campaigner in the Irish Free State general election that was held on 16 February 1932. He was a supporter of the pro-Treaty Cumann na nGaedheal (later Fine Gael) party, who were defeated by Fianna Fáil. They were old adversaries in the Civil War ten years earlier and there was political tension on both sides following the election, with tit-for-tat shootings being carried out. John possibly feared for his own safety.

On Good Friday, 25 March, Johanna Moran was returning to her home in Killinick from the local Catholic church in Ballymore. Passing the laneway leading up to the Cousins' house, she heard noises and observed Jane O'Brien at the hedge inside the gate with an implement in her hand. They wished each other a good day and Mrs Moran thought nothing further of it.

Jane's son, John O'Brien, left home at around six-thirty on Easter Saturday evening, 26 March, leaving John Cousins behind in the house. He cycled into Wexford and met his girlfriend Nellie O'Brien (no relation). They met up in Hayes' bicycle shop on South Main Street, where they left their bikes. This was the custom then for people coming into town. They each paid Thomas Hayes the threepence storage fee and went together to the cinema – either the Cinema Palace on Harper's Lane or the newly-opened Capitol Cinema. They later cycled together back to Nellie's house in Redmondstown, near Johnstown, and John continued home to Killinick. When he reached 'The Sanctuary' at about 1.20am, he came across John Cousins lying on the road badly injured, in great pain and surrounded by a group of people.

John Cousins had gone into the village to socialize in the home of his fiancée Nan Maguire. He left there at around 11.30pm accompanied by his friend and neighbour, James O'Reilly. They parted ways when they reached the gate into the laneway that led to the Cousins' house which, unusually, had been left open. Suddenly in the darkness there was a loud bang. James turned around to see John returning from inside the gateway holding his stomach and calling out "Jem, I'm shot!".

John collapsed and James dragged him off the roadway and laid him next to the gate of the Rowe family cottage on the far side of the road. He alerted Robert Rowe, then called to Father Murphy in Ballymore and got someone to

The entrance to the laneway leading to the Cousins' house, 'The Sanctuary', in Killinick. Jane O'Brien lay in wait on the right-hand side, just inside the gate behind the hedge, with a shotgun. As her nephew approached from the left in darkness, she shot him in the abdomen. (photo: Des Kiely)

Robert Rowe's cottage, seen on the right, lies opposite the entrance to the Cousins' laneway. John Cousins collapsed on the roadway after he was shot. His neighbour James O'Reilly pulled him in off the road and he lay for up to ninety minutes beside the entrance to the Rowe house. (photo: Des Kiely))

summon a doctor and the gardaí. Sergeant Patrick Hanley arrived by bicycle accompanied by another garda from Rosslare Strand garda barracks. Dr James Anglim, who travelled from Ballyregan, got to the scene just after the gardaí, at around one in the morning. They found the victim lying on his back on the side of the road in agony. He was covered with four or five coats that were saturated with blood. John had a four-inch gaping wound in the front of his abdomen. Dr Anglim treated him the best he could and directed that he be moved to the County Hospital in Wexford.

A car was found to convey him to hospital but it suffered a puncture on the way, which delayed them by about a half an hour. John was crying out and complaining of being in great pain on the six-mile journey to Wexford. By the time they reached the hospital he was dead.

The authorities first believed that the killing might have been political, involving the IRA, as they had been aware of John Cousins' campaigning during the recent election. But there had also been talk locally of animosity between John Cousins and his aunt.

At around 4.30am on Easter Sunday morning, during heavy rain, Garda Superintendent O'Halloran and Sergeant Hanley arrived back in Killinick. In the company of John O'Brien, they called to the Cousins' house. When his mother Jane opened the door, John told her that there had been an accident in the village. But she was already sobbing, without shedding any tears. "An accident, an accident!" responded Mrs O'Brien. "Was it a motor car? Poor John, what happened to him at all? Poor fellow." Sergeant Hanley carried out a search of John Cousins' room, thinking he might find threatening letters in connection with his political activity, but found nothing.

In the hours following the shooting, Richard Kelly, who owned land adjacent to the laneway where John Cousins was shot, noticed that a hawthorn bush in the hedging had been cut and left hanging. The bush was about seven yards in from the Cousins' entrance gate and would have offered a clear view of the gateway when pushed back. It appeared to have been recently cut with a fine saw. A saw with fresh sawdust particles was later retrieved by the gardaí from an outhouse at the rear of the Cousins' property.

Sergeant John Dwyer, while searching the area of the shooting, found the sealing cap of a shotgun cartridge inside the entrance gate to the Cousins' laneway. It lay in a straight line from where the bush was cut and the far pier of the gate. It was lying on the laneway, about eight feet from the gate pier.

A number of gardaí remained in the house all day. Later in the evening, Chief Superintendent McCarthy arrived in the company of Superintendent O'Halloran. McCarthy asked Jane O'Brien to accompany them upstairs to her bedroom and there he said to her: "We know all about it. We know the person who cut the bush in the lane where the shot was fired at John Cousins. You could save us the trouble of any further search and ease your mind." Mrs O'Brien stood at the foot of her bed and pointed to the centre. From under the mattress the Chief Superintendent removed a single-barrelled shotgun. It

Dr James Anglim, the local doctor from Ballyregan, who attended John Cousins at the scene of the shooting as well as the post-mortem that followed in Wexford County Hospital.

still smelled strongly of gunpowder and appeared to have been recently discharged. While still in the bedroom, Sergeant Hanley arrested O'Brien and charged her with the murder of her nephew. "I'll do the best I can for you," McCarthy reassured her. "What is going to happen to me at all?" she asked.

Jane O'Brien was taken to the garda barracks on Lower George's Street in Wexford – the former RIC barracks located on the corner of Abbey Street and now known as Pembroke House. While there, she dictated a letter to her sister in England, explaining the situation that she found herself in and claiming that her nephew had given her an ultimatum to be out of the house by Easter Saturday. She asked her to take care of her son John. Jane O'Brien was later removed to Waterford Jail.

A post-mortem was carried out on Easter Monday in Wexford County Hospital by the hospital surgeon, Dr Michael O'Brien. He was in the company of Dr Anglim and Chief Superintendent McCarthy. Pellets were removed from the body and kept by McCarthy as evidence.

THE TRIAL

The trial of Jane O'Brien opened before Judge John O'Byrne in the Central Criminal Court, Green Street, Dublin on Monday, 6 June 1932. All murder cases and other serious crimes were tried here. The trial lasted three days and attracted huge press attention nationally.

In the course of the trial, a handwriting expert, Captain Arthur Quirke, compared the writing on the malicious postcards received by Nan Maguire and John Cousins. It matched the entries found in the accused's diary and on blotting paper recovered by the gardaí from her bedroom. The word 'lovely' was misspelled as 'lovilly' on several of the postcards as well as in her diary. He also compared the handwriting to that in a letter written by Jane O'Brien to her son during her time in Waterford Jail.

The accused, Jane O'Brien in 1932, being escorted by gardaí to
Wexford Courthouse, then located within the grounds of Wexford Jail
on Spawell Road. (photo: The People newspaper)

Evidence was given by the victim's fiancée Nan Maguire of an incident that took place in Killinick Post Office in January. When Nan entered, Jane O'Brien was there but immediately left, saying to the postmistress: "I will have to go now unless Nan Maguire will think I am sending postcards." But neither Nan or her fiancé had mentioned the postcards to anyone.

Gun expert George Cooke of Cooke's Sporting Depot, 77 North Main Street, Wexford (now Empress boutique), testified. He was given possession of the shotgun found in the accused's bedroom and said that with it he fired a similar cartridge to that which was found at the scene of the shooting. He gave evidence that when he fired the gun, the particular characteristics of the resulting indent on the cap corresponded with those found on the spent cartridge.

On the final day of the trial, Joseph Carthy, solicitor for the State, addressing the jury of twelve men, concluded that the motive for the premeditated killing of John Cousins was to prevent him marrying Nan Maguire, which would have led to both herself and her son having to vacate the house.

After just one hour of deliberation, the jury found Jane O'Brien guilty of murder, with a rider recommending mercy, owing to her gender and age. From *The New Ross Standard* (10 June 1932): "Donning the black cap, His Lordship sentenced the accused to be executed on Thursday, June 30th."

The only woman hanged since the formation of the Free State in 1922 was County Limerick native Annie Walsh in 1925 for the murder of her husband. The 31st Eucharistic Congress was due to be held in Dublin on 22-26 June 1932. This was an assembly of bishops, priests and lay people from all parts of the world. The year was the 1,500th anniversary of the arrival of Saint Patrick in Ireland in AD432. The spectacle of having a woman hanged in Montjoy Jail within days of this major religious event was seen as unseemly by the Catholic Church. The Archbishop petitioned the State's Governor-General, James McNeill, who signed an order commuting Jane O'Brien's death sentence to penal servitude for life. She was released from prison in 1941, having served nine years, and was transferred to the Sisters of Charity.

Within those short few months, young John O'Brien's uncle died, his mother murdered his cousin and she faced the death penalty. 'The Sanctuary' lay empty and John was now left without a home.

Oylegate fishermen employed by Powers whiskey distillery

Edermine House, built in 1838 for John Power. It has been described as 'possibly the most interesting domestic architectural ensemble in County Wexford.' (photo: Robert French, NLI, late 1800s)

JOHN POWER, successor to the Powers whiskey distillery family business in Dublin, established the family seat at Edermine, about three miles south of Enniscorthy on the eastern side of the River Slaney. The family had a row of houses built in the nearby village of Oylegate in 1878 for local fishermen, who moved to Dublin for the winter months to work in the distillery and returned to their homes in summer for the salmon fishing season.

John Power's grandfather James, a Catholic innkeeper, began distilling his own whiskey at the rear of his premises on Thomas Street in Dublin in 1791. Due to its increased popularity, James established a larger distillery on nearby John's Lane. He married a Wexford woman, Mary Brennan, in 1799. On his death in 1817, he was succeeded by his son John and the company was now known as John Power & Son. Following the passing of the 1823 Excise Act that made stills legal on the payment of a licensing fee, the business flourished because within a decade almost all illegal stills had disappeared.

In County Wexford, Andrew Jameson, son of the famous John Jameson, set up a distillery at Fairfield outside Enniscorthy in 1818 and it produced whiskey into the early 1830s, when the building became part of Davis Flour Mills. Bishopswater Distillery was opened in 1827 by Nicholas Devereux and operated at its site on Distillery Road in Wexford town until 1914.

Sir John Power (1771-1855), who had Edermine House built in 1838.

John Power, whose mother was an Enniscorthy woman, purchased the Edermine Estate from Lawrence Toole in 1830. Toole was related to John Hyacinth Talbot of Ballytrent House. Talbot was MP for New Ross from 1832 to 1841 and his niece Maria was married to the 16th Earl of Shrewsbury, John Talbot of Alton Towers in Staffordshire. A close friend of the Earl was the architect and leading Gothic revivalist Augustus Welby Pugin. On a visit to Ballytrent in 1837, Pugin was given his first Irish commission by Talbot – the Church of the Assumption in Bree. Pugin also drew up plans for the reconstruction of John Power's house at Edermine for his only son James.

John Power was conferred with a baronetcy – an hereditary title – in 1841. A friend of Daniel O'Connell, who died in 1847, Sir John laid the foundation stone of the O'Connell round tower in Glasnevin Cemetery in 1854. His son, Sir James Power, married Jane, daughter of John Hyacinth Talbot in 1843. After the death of Talbot's young wife, Ann Eliza Redmond, in 1826, he wed James's sister Elizabeth Power in 1851.

When Sir John Power died in 1855 he was succeeded by his son James. Sir James Power had an address on Merrion Square, was Governor of the Bank of Ireland and was appointed High Sheriff of Dublin in 1859. He famously laid the foundation stone for the O'Connell Monument on Sackville Street in 1864. At the Chicago World's Fair in 1893, empty Powers whiskey bottles were used to produce a replica of the O'Connell round tower.

The impressive Edermine House and adjoining chapel today. (photo: Des Kiely)

EDERMINE HOUSE

View towards the back of the Pugin chapel showing the chancel screen, the decorated walls and roof and the high-level little windows from a bedroom in the house. (photo: Des Kiely)

Sir James and Lady Jane had a chapel built next to the house, designed by Augustus Pugin, who also designed nearby St. Aidan's Cathedral in Enniscorthy, its foundation stone laid in 1843. The Power family were benefactors, who paid towards the cathedral's construction.

Pugin's chapel at Edermine features a chancel screen – dividing the main body from the altar. The roof and walls are painted in a stencilled grid-like pattern, all preserved in their original state. An unusual small window high up at the back of the chapel could be opened into one of the bedrooms of the house, allowing an unwell person to follow the service.

Sir James Power also had a fine curvilinear cast-iron glasshouse with a central semi-dome erected near the house in 1860. Now in ruins, it was built by James Pierce of the Mill Road Iron Works, later Pierce's Foundry. It resembles the conservatory that he built at Castlebridge House two years earlier. The design has been attributed to the renowned glasshouse designer Richard Turner.

The ruined cast-iron glasshouse built by James Pierce in 1860, with overgrown vinery visible on the left. (photo: Des Kiely)

OYLEGATE

The village of Oylegate lies about two miles south of Edermine House on the main Enniscorthy to Wexford road. Formerly called Mullinagore, it gets its name from the Irish *Bearna na hAille*. The name means 'the gap in the cliff', from the gap through which the nearby River Slaney flows.

In the 1850s, the Power family offered much-needed winter employment to the men of Oylegate at the distillery in Dublin, when the distilling business was at its busiest after the barley harvest. Many of these local men were engaged in net fishing on the Slaney in the summer months. In this post-Famine period work was scarce and this would have been an attractive proposition. Travel was later possible by train on the west side of the river on the Dublin-Wexford line, using Macmine Station, which opened in 1873. A small station, Edermine Ferry, opened while Sir James Power was chairman of the Dublin, Wicklow & Wexford Railway. Both stations closed in 1964.

Sir James died in 1877 and was succeeded at Edermine by his eldest son, Sir John Talbot Power (1845-1901). The distillery was left to his younger sons James and Thomas. In 1878 the Power family had a row of houses, known as Powers Range, built for some of their employees in the village, which are still

The village of Oylegate circa 1900. (photo: Robert French, NLI)

The terrace of houses known as Powers Range in Oylegate. Constructed for the Power Whiskey distillery workers in 1878, the family coat of arms features above each door. (photo: Des Kiely)

occupied today and bear the Power family coat of arms. Additional homes known as the Lower Range were added in 1895. The rent was set at fourpence per week and in 1930 the tenants were given the option to buy out their homes for £28. Trips to the RDS Winter Fair in 1896 were organized by the Powers for local farmers, giving them the opportunity to learn about the latest innovations in agriculture. The distillery employed about 300 people in Dublin, and it is estimated that half of them came from the Oylegate area. One of the concessions to the men working in the distillery was that each was allowed two glasses of whiskey per day. Many settled in the Liberties and married locally, adding to the mix of the local inner-city accent, with some of the Dublin wives moving to live in Oylegate. The Oylegate men working in Powers later formed their own hurling team – the Father Murphy Hurling Club – and played in the Inter-Firm hurling league. The team trained in the Phoenix Park and in 1952 won the Miller Shield in the Dublin Junior Championship.

The entrance to John's Lane Distillery in Dublin.

It was customary at the time for distilleries to sell their produce directly to merchants and bonders, who in turn bottled it themselves. In 1886 John Power & Son became one of the first distilleries in the world to start bottling its own whiskey. Each bottle was given a gold label, giving their whiskey the name *Powers Gold Label*. In 1900, they introduced the miniature *Baby Power* – another first in the industry. They also led the trade by introducing various other sizes of bottles.

Sir John Talbot Power of Edermine was MP for County Wexford, 1868-74. He married Frances, daughter of Captain Henry Segrave of Kiltimon House, Newcastle, County Wicklow in 1876 and was appointed High Sheriff in 1880. Their son, Sir James Talbot Power, who had no children, succeeded to the Wexford estates in 1901. Sir Thomas Talbot Power, who died in 1930, was the last of the barons and the last family member to sit on the company board.

Powers embraced the change in consumer preference when they began to produce blended whiskey in 1961. They joined Cork Distillers and rivals John Jameson & Son to form Irish Distillers in 1966 with a single distillery in Midleton, County Cork. The John's Lane Distillery ceased operation in 1976, ending the company's working arrangement between Oylegate and Dublin. Some of the buildings and three whiskey stills, now protected structures, form part of Dublin's National College of Art and Design complex.

BENEDICTINE MONKS

The first pedestrian bridge at Edermine was constructed of timber and opened in 1898, connecting the parishes of Oylegate-Glenbrien on the east bank of the Slaney and Bree-Ballyhogue on the west. Marmion Bridge, a new vehicular single-lane crossing, was completed in 1975 and named after the Benedictine monk, Dom Columba Marmion. He was born Joseph Marmion in Smithfield in Dublin in 1858. He became abbot of Maredsous Abbey near Namur in Belgium, from where he fled at the outbreak of the First World War and established his Irish house at Edermine. He was beatified by Pope John Paul II in 2000.

Joseph Marmion was ordained in Rome in 1881 and five years later joined the Benedictine monks at Maredsous, taking the name Columba after the Irish saint. In 1899 he helped to found the Abbey of Mont César in Louvain and became its first prior. Having a deeply spiritual religious faith, Dom Columba

Dom Columba Marmion, who took refuge in Edermine House for the duration of the First World War.

Marmion was an inspiring teacher and in demand to give retreats throughout Belgium. In 1909 he was elected abbot of Maredsous Abbey, which had a community consisting of about one hundred monks. Fearing that his young novices might be conscripted after Germany invaded Belgium at the outbreak of the First World War in 1914, he decided to move them to safety in Ireland. Marmion travelled through the war zone disguised as a cattle dealer and without papers to England, and from there to County Wexford.

Edermine with its chapel was at the time in the temporary possession of a Father Nolan. The priest offered the house to the Benedictine monks, about sixteen of them, who sought refuge for the duration of the war. They arrived at Edermine in 1915 and remained there until the war ended and left in 1919. Local man Martin Doyle of nearby Rochfort House was an altar server in the chapel at the time. Edermine House had several owners over the following decades until the present owner, Martin Doyle's son Pat, bought it in 1977. Pat tells the story of a night in 1923 when his grandmother, who had known Dom Marmion, woke to find the monk standing in her bedroom before disappearing. She later learned that the Dom had died that very day in Belgium.

When the community of monks left at the end of the war they were remembered for miracles they had performed while in County Wexford. It was said that many people were cured at Edermine during the Spanish flu pandemic of 1918-19. A cure from cancer, reported by a woman from Minnesota in the USA who had visited Dom Marmion's tomb at Maredsous Abbey in 1963, led to his beatification in 2000 by Pope John Paul II after the case was investigated by the Church and deemed to be a miracle.

In 2019, Irish Distillers donated the records from the Power family's Edermine estate to Wexford County Archive. They include valuable information that details the history of the Powers' contribution to life in the county over many decades.

'Walked 10,000 miles through China to find his wife and child!'

Dr George Hadden was erroneously reported in 'The Day Book' to have been reunited with his wife Helen and son Patrick after a three-year search for them.

THE SHORT-LIVED tabloid newspaper, *The Day Book*, published in Chicago from 1911-17, contained lots of sensational content. One particular fantastical article that appeared in its edition of 13 March 1914 involved Wexfordman Dr George Hadden. Under the headline '*Walked 10,000 Miles Through China Wilds Searching For Lost Wife And Child*', this is the complete article:

'*Wandering for three years through the wildest parts of Central China in search of his wife and child, Dr. George Hadden, a missionary from Ireland, encountered adventures that rival fiction. In his hunt he covered 10,000 miles, traversed Hu-nan province to the border of Tibet, was pelted with clods by 2,000 semi-barbarous Chinese at Kuelyangchow and had many thrilling escapes from death.*

'*The Haddens were stationed at the mission of Yungchowfu, where he has been the missionary for seven years, and they were separated in March, 1910, by the Shangsha [Changsha] riots on the Yang [Xiang] river, a tributary of the Yangtse Kiang. Mrs. Hadden was carried to Hankow [Wuhan], where on St. Patrick's Day she gave birth to a boy. Dr. Hadden was carried up the river and so lost all knowledge of his wife's whereabouts and did not know about the child until he found them both, after three years of wandering, in Hongkong. He wrote many letters, none of which brought him news of his wife, and having no other method of travel he walked from place to place through the great interior of the empire. Dr. Hadden is a picturesque character in appearance, 7 feet 4 inches tall, and a great pedestrian. While walking across the plowed fields at Kuel Yang*

Chow, the natives, who are almost wild and uncivilized, looked upon him as a devil in flesh and blood, and followed him, 2,000 strong. He felt that to run would be to invite destruction, so he walked calmly before the excited horde, but admitted he walked rather fast. After three years of travel he finally got back to his old station in Yung Chow Fu and there learned that his wife was in Hongkong, where he joined her and for the first time saw his boy, who had been named Patrick by Mrs. Hadden because he was born March 17. They went to Canton, and are now going to their home in Ireland on a leave of absence. They will return to China.'

The story was reproduced in other publications across the United States. But such exaggerations were unnecessary. Dr George Hadden was indeed an extraordinary man with truly fascinating stories to tell. Yes, he was very tall – six feet four inches in height. The true narrative is that in 1910, Dr George Hadden, a medical missionary working in China, took his wife, Dr Helen, from Yungchowfu in south-central China north to Hankow (Wuhan) to escape rioting. She was in the home of Dr Robert Booth, a relative of the Haddens, when their first child, Patrick, was born. George had to return to Yungchowfu before Patrick's birth. His circumstances were unknown, until he returned to Hankow and his family after some weeks. They had two more children, also born in China; Ben in 1916 and Peg in 1919.

THE HADDEN FAMILY

The Haddens were members of the Methodist community, so named for 'the methodical way in which they carried out their Christian faith.' John Wesley founded Methodism in the 1700s. He visited Ireland on numerous occasions and established classes and societies throughout the country. He is said to have preached in the newly-constructed Market House (Wexford Arts Centre) shortly after it opened in 1776. The Wesleyan Methodist Chapel on Rowe Street in Wexford town was built in 1838, and closed in 1973.

Dr George Hadden was born in 1882 at Richmond Terrace, Spawell Road. His great-grandfather, Reverend John Hadden (1778-1842), was a Wesleyan Methodist minister. George's grandfather, also George, established the drapery business, Hadden's, on North Main Street, Wexford in 1848, opposite his brother John's pharmacy, Hadden's Medical Hall. After the death of George from tuberculosis at the young age of 33, the business was run by his wife, Frances, who was widowed with four young children. After seventeen years

Large crowd gathered for a 1926 sale at Hadden's Drapery (far right, now Shaw's). At the time the shop was run by brothers William and George (the father of Dr George Hadden). Their uncle John Hadden owned the Medical Hall (centre). (photo courtesy Helen Masterson)

at the helm, she passed it on to her eldest sons William and George in 1875. The shop was then known as W. & G. Hadden.

That George married Hannah Perrott in 1881 and they had eight children: four boys and four girls. The eldest was Dr George Hadden. In 1897, the family moved to Springfield House, close to the County Infirmary on Hill Street, where a cousin, Dr David Hadden, was the chief physician. Their father, George senior, was one of the founders of the Wexford Hat Company in 1903. W. & G. Hadden expanded their drapery business into Dungarvan in 1906 and Carlow in 1909. George senior was very active in local politics and a member of Wexford Corporation for forty years. William went blind, as did his brother George in later life, and bowed out of the family business in 1914. He passed away two years later.

Of the eight children, George, Richard and Marie all became medical doctors, while the younger sons William and Addison went into the drapery business. George attended the Tate School (later the Municipal Building, and now part of the new Wexford Courthouse). He was subsequently educated in the Methodist secondary school, Wesley College, St Stephen's Green, Dublin.

CHINA MISSIONS

George enrolled at Edinburgh University, graduating with a Bachelor of Medicine and Surgery degree in 1905. It was there that he met fellow medical student and his future wife, Helen Vickers, of the Vickers Oils family in

Leeds. In 1906, they both travelled to China to serve as Methodist medical missionaries.

The so-called Second Opium War – between the British and the French against the Qing dynasty of China – ended in 1860 with the signing of several treaties. Christian missionary activity was now permitted beyond Canton to the entire country and missionary activity in China increased dramatically. Thousands of foreigners arrived with their families to spread Christianity, establish schools and work as medical missionaries. Among them were George and Helen. George developed a small hospital in Yungchowfu, Hunan province, in south-central China. Helen began work at the Margaret Bennett Hospital in Wuchang (Wuhan). Despite her lack of knowledge of the language, she filled the vacancy caused by the death of the hospital's founder, Margaret Bennett in 1906. Dr George and Dr Helen married in Changsha in 1909 and Helen joined her husband in Yungchowfu.

George's younger brother, Richard, and sister, Marie, also studied medicine. Richard graduated from Trinity in 1908 and travelled to China in 1911 to serve in the Methodist missions. Marie graduated in 1916 and first went to China in 1927. Richard worked in the southern cities of Foshan and Wuzhou. He became fluent in Chinese and was known in the country as Dr Ma Zuosheng. Richard took a break from his medical missionary work during the First World War and joined the British Royal Army Medical Corps,

Dr George and Dr Helen Hadden were based in Yungchowfu. Dr Richard Hadden died in Zhaotung.

becoming captain, and saw action in Gallipoli, Palestine, Egypt, France and Flanders. He returned to China in 1919 and was based in the north-eastern province of Shandong. After ten years, he was transferred to Zhaotong, in Yunnan province, to fill a mission vacancy. There, he contracted typhoid at the hospital where he was working and died in 1930, having refused a life-saving injection that was in short supply, saying it should be administered to a patient who might be more severely infected. Marie worked as a doctor in China from 1927 and married Vincent S. Hamill, Shanghai harbour master. Until 1941, she was a school medical officer in Shanghai, before returning to Ireland after the Second World War.

During the First World War, Dr George Hadden travelled to Siberia in 1917 and 1918, assisting the American Red Cross Mission war effort to aid refugees of the Bolshevik fighting. He joined the medical staff in hospitals and clinics at points along the Trans-Siberian Railway. In the Ural Mountains he came into contact with the Czechoslovak Legion, who were fighting Lenin's Bolsheviks. There, he apparently met a Czechoslovakian soldier who was once employed as a waiter in Killarney. Later, when recounting his time in Russia, he would tell people how he commuted to work every day on the Trans-Siberian Railway.

Back in China, Dr Hadden was working with the Methodist mission for the Chinese Medical Association. In 1923, he founded the Institute of Hospital Technology in Anqing, which three years later moved to Hankow, now part of the city of Wuhan, where the Han river meets the Yangtze. (Hankow, Wuchang and Hanyang merged to become Wuhan city in 1949). The institute was the first mission-run school for medical technicians in China to provide training in x-ray and laboratory techniques. Dr Hadden was in charge of the institute for ten years, until 1933. It merged with the Union Hospital the following year.

In China, Dr Hadden refused to wear a sun helmet, which he associated with Victorian colonial rule. Despite warnings from his colleagues, he preferred not to wear a hat at all. He once walked thirty miles a day for nine days without any protection from the sun.

While working in China, he contracted the then little understood chronic tropical disease, sprue, which affects the digestive system and can result in extreme weight loss. It was believed to be fatal and Dr Hadden travelled to London in 1923 for treatment. He was advised not to return to China, but did, and within a few months had to go back to London. From there he moved to

Dr George Hadden in 1930, when he headed up the Institute of Hospital Technology in Hankow (Wuhan) and (right) with students of the institute. (photos courtesy Yvonne Hadden)

the Channel Islands to convalesce. But the ever-restless doctor made several trips back to the mainland. On one occasion the ferry for Southampton ran onto rocks leaving St Helier and was wrecked. He managed to get off and made his way to dry land by clambering over rocks. And so Dr Hadden could later tell the tale of how he was one of the few people who walked ashore from a shipwreck. He finally overcame the mysterious sprue disease.

Perhaps the worst natural disaster of the twentieth century occurred in August 1931 when the Yangtze River, the third longest in the world, burst its banks and flooded a 500-square-mile area following prolonged heavy rainfalls. The rice fields that dominated the landscape were swamped, destroying the crop. Cities such as Wuhan and Nanjing depended on this rice and, without it, inhabitants starved to death. The polluted river also resulted in outbreaks of cholera, typhoid and dysentery. The estimated 3.7 million people who died from this flood, over the next several months, perished from starvation and disease, many after the flood waters had receded.

The newly-built Hankow Union Hospital, where George was working, was flooded to a depth of over fifteen feet. In a letter home to the family in Wexford he wrote of his experience in the house of one of the nurses, Sister Gladys Stephenson: *'At lunchtime I went to swim in Sister's house to rescue her curtains which we had piled over the poles downstairs. It was a queer sensation. The faint glimmer of light over the tops of the windows gave a ghostly effect in the place, while the electric bulbs hanging from the ceiling were afloat. A teapot was afloat and lots of pictures, as well as such heavy furniture as had been left there.'* Along with colleagues, Dr

Hadden treated cholera patients in camps of small tents erected on high ground and at points along the Han river. Five refugee camps were established and mass graves had to be dug, one at each camp, to bury the victims.

Both brothers, George and Richard, were awarded various robes and scrolls by their grateful Chinese patients. These have been in storage for decades in the National Museum of Ireland and are held in the Decorative Arts & History section of Collins Barracks.

In 2020, the Union Hospital became one of the first designated hospitals to treat patients suffering from Covid-19 in Wuhan, where the first known human cases of the disease were recorded.

RETURN TO WEXFORD

In 1933, during George's last days in China, Helen was in England when she was involved in a serious motorcycle accident in Coventry. Ben, their son, was driving, while she rode in the sidecar. In the crash, she was not seriously injured, but tragically he was killed. George received the news as he prepared to sail from Shanghai and could not attend the funeral or burial in Coventry. It was a heart-breaking loss. George retired from the Methodist Missionary Society in 1934. Thereafter, Helen and he rented a house on St John's Road.

George became involved in his brother Addison's furniture enterprise. As well as managing Hadden's drapery shop in Wexford, Addison had established the Slaney Furniture Manufacturing Company. For his first two years back in Wexford, George focused on the building of a Snipe class racing dinghy, which he introduced to the Wexford Boat Club.

His last period of medical mission work was in Nigeria from mid-1936 to early 1938. He had been invited to join a hospital that catered for a sub-tribe of the Igbo people. While based there he made frequent visits to a nearby leper colony, where he helped out in any way he could. Stories from his time in west Africa included adventures by canoe along the Niger River. He also visited his niece Maureen Hadden, also a Methodist missionary, and her husband Rev. Richard Morris, in Gold Coast (now Ghana). On that trip, he included a visit to Elmina Castle, once used as a slave depot by European slave traders. He also followed in the wake of the 19th century Scottish explorer, Mungo Park, by riding the Bussa rapids on the Niger, where Park met his fate in 1806. Being an avid reader of history and travel books, including the adventure novel *Beau*

Geste, George was prompted to journey north through the French territory of Niger to the Foreign Legion's last outpost in southern Sahara.

Now retired from medicine, George and Helen settled permanently in Wygram House on Davitt Road in 1939. The house directly faces his old centre of learning, the former Tate School. George's father had died in 1925 and his mother Hannah passed away in 1940. He soon became very active in the community, socially and politically. W. & G. Hadden provided income for George and his other siblings through the shares that they held in the business.

A lasting institution that he founded in 1941 was the Wexford Male Voice Choir. He had sung himself in the university choir while studying in Edinburgh, all those years ago, and he now formed part of the bass section. In 1943, he became governor of the Tate School and remained in that position until it closed in 1948. It was transformed into the Municipal Buildings the following year. As governor, he was involved in recruiting new students, taught the school choir and also supervised the cooking.

Among the many skills that Dr Hadden possessed was how to fire bricks, an expertise he acquired in China, and how to dry clothes in sub-zero temperatures – something he learned in Siberia. He was an active board

member of An Óige, the Irish Youth Hostel Association, and served as vice-president. Having numerous hobbies, he was also involved in the Wexford Cage Bird Society and was patron of the Wexford United Pigeon Flying Club.

The author, Patrick Semple, writing in his memoirs about growing up in Wexford, remembers his father renting a portion of the back garden of the Haddens house at Wygram, to grow vegetables. The entrance was through a garage door opposite the Vallotton monument. In the garage sat their Morris Eight car, up on blocks, for the duration of the war. Patrick would play in it as his father worked in the vegetable plot. He recalls once taking a lift after the war from Dr Helen, who was hard of hearing: '*She once gave me a lift from Avenue de Flandre to the Bullring*

Dr George Hadden (without socks) at Carnsore Point in 1963. (photo courtesy Yvonne Hadden)

and handed me her huge ear trumpet to mind while she drove. She explained to me how she was always glad when a pedestrian was crossing the end of a street she was passing as it indicated to her that no car was coming down that street that could collide with her. I felt it polite to respond to what she was saying but she couldn't hear a word I said as her ear trumpet was on my knee. Dr Helen couldn't reverse. When she called on a particular friend on Spawell Road she had to continue as far as Carcur and turn right back to town, doing a circuit to get home.' On George, Semple wrote: *'He used a bicycle which had a motor fitted on the back carrier with a drive to the back wheel. He didn't use the motor going down town as it was all downhill. He was a big man and he put the motor to the test as it put-put-putted up Hill Street on his way home.'*

Dr Hadden encouraged others who shared his interest in local and medieval history and archaeology. In 1944, he founded the Old Wexford Society (later known as the Wexford Historical Society) with T. D. Sinnott, former Wexford County Manager, Rev. Timothy Nolan, President of St Peter's College, and others. He was a man of great intellect and wrote regularly on the town's origins and heritage and the county's railway and gave numerous monthly society lectures. When the Wexford Festival Opera started in 1951, Dr Hadden instigated guided walking tours of the town during the annual international festival. He continued as chairman of the Historical Society until 1971. In recognition, its Dr George Hadden Memorial Lecture is held annually during Wexford Festival Opera.

Cycling one day towards Glendalough, George's mind wandered back to the French Foreign Legion and the amazing distances they marched in a single day. He remembered a quote from *Beau Geste*: *'…cleaning materials, soap and towels, but no socks, for the Legion does not wear them.'* Hadden pondered this for a while and then dismounted. He removed his socks and from that day never wore them again. The tall, white-haired, long-bearded Dr Hadden is still affectionately remembered by many, walking through Wexford town, hands behind his back and without socks or overcoat, even in winter. The windows of their house in Wygram were kept open throughout the year for air circulation. If they ever had surplus hot water, Dr Hadden was known to offer a stranger the use of their bath. On summer evenings, his wife is remembered sitting on a chair in the street at the front door under an umbrella for shade.

Like his father before him, Dr Hadden, a civic-minded man who wanted to serve the community, was active in local politics. He was the only Protestant on Wexford Corporation when he joined and went on to become an Alderman. In 1972, he was honoured by being made the 18th recipient of the Freedom of the Borough of Wexford, the ceremony taking place in the Town Hall in Cornmarket. Conferring the doctor with the highest honour, Mayor Des Corish said: *'I feel privileged to pay tribute to one of nature's gentlemen... a man who adored every street and lane of the rock from which he was born. The name of Dr George Hadden will be remembered in Wexford...and well he deserves to be remembered.'*

A year later, Dr George Hadden died, aged 90. His funeral service was held in the Methodist Church on Rowe Street, the last ever before the church shut its doors for good that same year. It was attended by the Mayor, and the Wexford Male Voice Choir sang and also acted as a guard of honour. The Corporation arranged a public funeral procession for the much respected and charitable native of the town. His coffin, draped in the municipal flag, was taken down Rowe Street and Anne Street and along the quays as it made its way to Crosstown Cemetery. The streets were lined with hundreds of residents and shops on the route closed as a mark of respect.

In 1971, he asked that when the time came for his epitaph to be written, the author simply record, *'He refused to grow old'*. His wife, Helen, received the traditional cheque from President Hillery on her 100th birthday in 1980. When she passed away, aged 103, in 1983, she was the oldest resident at the time in Wexford.

Grateful thanks to Yvonne Hadden for her assistance in compiling this story.

Dr George Hadden in 1971 with the Wexford artist, Phoebe Donovan, who painted his portrait. It was presented to George by the Old Wexford Society to mark his retirement from the historical society that he founded. (photo courtesy Yvonne Hadden)

Parnell and Redmond: Victorian betrayal and loyalty

Charles Stewart Parnell   *Katharine O'Shea*   *John Redmond*

THE AFFAIR between the Irish Parliamentary Party leader and a married woman shocked the Victorian political establishment. Parnell's divorce in 1890 turned the Catholic clergy in Ireland against him and resulted in a split in the National Land League. But Wexfordman John Redmond, a fervent admirer of Charles Stewart Parnell, stood by him and after his premature death a year later, replaced him as leader of the party.

Parnell was born in Rathdrum, County Wicklow in 1846. His father John was from a wealthy Anglo-Irish Anglican landowning family and his mother was American-born Delia Stewart. She was the daughter of Admiral Charles Stewart, an American naval hero who, in his first commission in the US Navy, served on the USS *United States* under its captain, Wexford native John Barry. William Parnell, his grandfather, was a Liberal MP for Wicklow in 1817-20.

In 1870, the Home Government Association was launched by the Donegal-born barrister and parliamentarian Isaac Butt in support of Home Rule for Ireland. In 1874, the pressure group became a full political party: the Home Rule Party. Charles Stewart Parnell was elected its MP for Meath in 1875. The Home Rule Party was represented in Wexford at the time by William Redmond, father of John Redmond, who would become leader of what ultimately became the Irish Parliamentary Party.

Parnell leaned more towards the radical element of the Home Rule Party and Fenian sentiments. In the House of Commons in 1876 he said he did not believe that the three Fenians publicly hanged in Manchester in 1867 in front of up to 10,000 people for the killing of a policeman had committed murder. He became heavily involved in 'obstructionism' – the practice of giving lengthy speeches which were off-topic in order to focus attention on Irish issues. This tactic was opposed by Butt who favoured a less hardline approach in parliament.

Back in Ireland Parnell held platform meetings, speaking to poor tenant farmers whose landlords were demanding excessive rents. He told them: *'You must show the landlord that you intend to keep a firm grip on your homesteads and lands. You must not allow yourselves be dispossessed as you were dispossessed in 1847'* – referring to the half-a-million people evicted in that year. The Irish National Land League was founded in 1879 by Michael Davitt, and Parnell was elected as its president. The movement was established to end excessive rents, prevent evictions and obtain ownership of the land by tenant farmers.

The Land League's 'land war' spread throughout the country. Apart from the abolition of landlordism, the League promoted the belief that the land rightfully belonged to the Irish people and had been stolen by the British. This helped to politicize rural Ireland and Parnell saw land agitation as a means of ultimately gaining Home Rule. William Redmond's son Willie, younger brother of John, joined the Land League.

Land League poster from 1882 calling for the non-payment of rents, while Parnell, Dillon and Willie Redmond sat in jail.

Meanwhile, in the 1880 general election 64 members of the Home Rule Party were elected to the House of Commons, including 27 supporters of Parnell, who was then nominated the new party leader. Gladstone was again Prime Minister and under the Land Act 1881, a Land Commission was established to confront the land question in Ireland. The Act was criticized by Parnell, Willie Redmond and others, who were arrested for possession of 'seditious literature' and imprisoned for three months in Kilmainham Jail, where they shared the same cell. While in prison, they called on tenant farmers in their *'No Rent Manifesto'* to stop paying rent. This resulted in the Land League being outlawed.

Home Rule MP William O'Shea, first husband of Katharine Wood.

The Liberal government secretly negotiated with Parnell while he was in jail. They sent the MP for Clare, William O'Shea as its intermediary. After six hours of discussions, Parnell tacitly agreed to support the government if released. The concession O'Shea won, the so-called *Kilmainham Treaty*, is believed to have been achieved after he threatened Parnell with exposing his secret affair with O'Shea's estranged wife, Katharine.

Born in Dublin and Catholic, William O'Shea was a captain in the British Army. In 1867, he married Katharine Wood, daughter of Sir John Wood, who became a Church of England vicar in Essex. Captain O'Shea was dashing and handsome but the couple had financial problems and William was abroad most of the time. Though they had three children together in the first seven years of their marriage, the couple grew further apart in the 1870s. Her husband was rumoured to have had numerous affairs and Katharine became more isolated.

In the 1880 general election, O'Shea won a seat as an Independent Nationalist for County Clare. The Home Rule Party, then led by William Shaw, was the largest party in Ireland, taking two-thirds of the seats. William O'Shea was keen to pursue an association with Parnell following his election success. In the summer of 1880, with Katharine by his side for appearance's sake, he introduced her to Parnell at Westminster. The couple were already living apart. He had her convince Parnell to attend a dinner party at her home, Wonersh Lodge in Eltham, southeast London.

A relationship quickly developed between Katie, as she was known, and Charles. They were both 34 years old. He was called 'the uncrowned king of Ireland' and he gave her the name 'Queenie'. This was the Victorian era, where different sets of rules

Katharine O'Shea, who conducted a ten-year relationship with Parnell before they married.

John Redmond's first wife, Australian-born Johanna (née Dalton).

applied to married men and women. It was thought that the man's fidelity should not matter, whereas a woman's infidelity was grounds for divorce.

After all the Kilmainham Jail internees were released, and with the Land League outlawed, Parnell simply announced a new organization called the National League in 1882. Parnell, Davitt and Willie Redmond travelled together on a hugely successful fundraising trip to the United States. The following year, Willie and his brother John visited Australia to raise funds for the cause. While there they met cousins Eleanor and Johanna Dalton, who were to become their future wives.

John Redmond hoped to inherit his father's Wexford seat when he died in 1880. He wrote to Parnell requesting the seat but Parnell had already offered it to his protégé Timothy Healy instead. The following year, however, in a by-election in New Ross, Redmond, now 24, was elected unopposed as a Parnellite. In his maiden speech in the House of Commons, which coincided with the arrest of the Land League leader, Michael Davitt, he was ejected from the house. John's brother Willie took his father's old seat in Wexford in 1883.

The National League had the endorsement of the Catholic Church and Parnell led a disciplined Home Rule movement with the new party name, the Irish Parliamentary Party, from 1882. He was now at the height of his political career. John Redmond, a devoted follower of Parnell, became party whip. Prime Minister Gladstone introduced the first Home Rule Bill in 1886 but it was defeated. The Bill created fear among the Protestant and Unionist communities. This resulted in riots in Belfast in which many died and the Orange Order was revived to resist Home Rule.

During the second half of the 1880s, Parnell continued to push for Home Rule. He risked a political scandal, however, if his affair with O'Shea's wife was made public and they managed to keep it under wraps for a decade. Charles and Katharine had three daughters in quick succession between 1882 and 1884. Their first born, Sophie, died at only two months old.

John and Willie Redmond married the Dalton cousins in 1883. John and Johanna had three children but she died prematurely six years later, aged only 28, after giving birth to a stillborn daughter. He was devastated by her death and withdrew from public life for about a year.

William Gladstone's failed Home Rule Bill resulted in a split in the Liberal Party and the collapse of the government. Timothy Healy conceived the Plan of Campaign in the same year. The Land Act of 1881 meant that in times of poor harvest, tenant farmers could have their rent reduced by about a quarter. But the Irish National League advocated withholding excessive rent payments to landlords. The new Conservative government outlawed the Campaign, declaring it to be 'an unlawful and criminal conspiracy.'

The violence that ensued around the country led to Parnell disassociating himself from the agrarian conflict. John Redmond, though by no means a radical, supported the Campaign, declaring its purpose was *'to win rent reductions and avert mass evictions'*. He also saw that by supporting the conflict it might retain the people's support for the Irish Parliamentary Party.

In 1886, a by-election for Galway city was called. Parnell proposed William O'Shea to stand as an Independent. The MP Timothy Healy and other leading members of the Irish Parliamentary Party, who knew of Parnell's relationship with O'Shea's estranged wife, voiced their opposition to the nomination. They believed that by putting his personal relationship first he was endangering the future of the party and risking a scandal. Parnell knew that Healy, formerly one of his greatest supporters, had long planned to betray him and insisted

Parnell, with bandaged head, had now fallen from grace. On the campaign trail for the North Kilkenny by-election in 1890, he had quicklime thrown in his eye.

on O'Shea's nomination. Despite William O'Shea winning the seat, a rift had now opened up within the party.

Katharine O'Shea and her estranged husband William were in line to inherit the estate of Katharine's very wealthy aunt, her mother's sister, Mrs. Benjamin Wood. But when she passed away in 1889, she left her estate in trust to Katharine. The will was contested by her siblings and overturned, giving equal share to each of them. This is just one of the many theories as to why Captain O'Shea filed for divorce in December of that year. But over the years O'Shea and Parnell had many political differences and any of these could have been the reason.

William O'Shea publicly named Parnell as his wife's lover, charged her with adultery and filed for divorce in December 1889. There followed a frenzy of newspaper coverage and the divorce case was to become one of the most notorious sex scandals of the Victorian era. Parnell's behaviour was seen as immoral and abhorrent. In the British press, Katharine was dubbed 'Kitty' O'Shea – a term used at the time for a prostitute.

Parnell believed he could survive the controversy and would be supported by the people of Ireland. But Gladstone, who was in discussions with Parnell on a new Home Rule bill, told him that if he continued as leader of the Irish Parliamentary Party the bill would be withdrawn. The party that represented many of the Irish people at Westminster was split. In order to preserve the alliance with Gladstone's Liberal Party, 44 voted against Parnell with 27 supporting him. The 'pro-Parnellites' led by John Redmond, who remained loyal to the 'chief', formed the breakaway Irish National League. The 'anti-Parnellites' under John Dillon formed the Irish National Federation.

The divorce was heard over two days in November 1890 and Parnell was not represented in court. Katharine accused her husband of wilful neglect and encouraging and facilitating her affair with Parnell in order to further his own interests. She said he would get her to ask favours of Parnell that would benefit him politically. Katharine also named numerous women, including her own sister Anna, with whom he was unfaithful. William O'Shea was granted the divorce on the grounds of his wife's infidelity and the court awarded custody of Katharine and Charles' two surviving daughters to her ex-husband.

The Catholic Church in Ireland spoke out against Parnell and this helped sway public opinion, especially in rural areas. In the various by-elections of

1891 the Catholic clergy strongly supported the anti-Parnellites faction and were opposed to John Redmond's Irish National League side.

Charles and Katharine married secretly in June 1891 in a Brighton registry office, having been refused a church wedding. The only witnesses were two servants from Katharine's house in Hove, near Brighton. The Catholic Church was shocked by the breaking of the vows of her previous marriage. Parnell continued to campaign back in Ireland in the third and last by-election of that year in County Carlow. His last days were spent travelling back and forth between Ireland and Brighton. But he was suffering from stress and exhaustion and his health was in decline. Just four months after the wedding he died, aged only 45, at home in Katharine's arms.

His loyal supporter, John Redmond, organized Parnell's funeral, reported to have been attended by 200,000. His coffin was placed in a wooden crate and taken by train to Holyhead and across to Kingstown. On arrival at Westland Row station, the outer casing was removed and a number of the assembled crowd eagerly grabbed pieces of it as souvenirs. Thousands lined the streets of Dublin along the route to Glasnevin Cemetery on Sunday, 11 October 1891. The procession moved slowly and the absence of any priests was conspicuous. Katharine did not travel to Ireland for her husband's funeral. In fact she never set foot on Irish soil despite having been married to two Irishmen. After Parnell's death, she suffered from a nervous breakdown and disappeared from public life. She died aged 75 in 1921.

Parnell's death affected John Redmond deeply. He resigned his North Wexford seat in order to contest Parnell's now-vacant Cork City seat, but was defeated by anti-Parnellite Martin Flavin. He ran the following month in another by-election to represent Waterford City. It was a bitter battle against anti-Parnellite Michael Davitt, who had the backing of the local Catholic clergy, but Redmond won the seat comfortably.

John Redmond lacked Parnell's charisma and oratory skills, however, and was not considered as having outstanding capacity for leadership. In

Mrs Katharine Parnell in 1914.

the general election of 1892, he was left with only ten followers out of eighty-five Home Rulers in Westminster. Yet Redmond continued his fight for Home Rule and the repeal of the Act of Union of 1800. But unlike Parnell, he did not seek separation from the British Empire. *'To talk about Ireland separating from the Empire,'* he declared, *'is the most utter nonsense.'* Redmond sought self-government for Ireland but with Imperialist interests safeguarded. He came from a professional Catholic landowning family that remained faithful to the British Crown.

With the rejection of the second Home Rule Bill in 1893, Gladstone retired from public life. Ireland entered a comparatively peaceful period. There were improvements in agricultural methods and farmers' co-ops were established, led by notable reformers such as Sir Horace Plunkett and George Russell. In 1894, the Irish Agricultural Organization Society was formed, with Plunkett as its first president. The Gaelic League, founded in 1893, revived an interest in the Irish language, music, dance and sports in towns and remote villages throughout the country.

John Redmond joined Plunkett's so-called Recess Committee in Parliament that brought together men of the landlord class as well as farmers and merchants with the aim of improving life in Ireland. The development of agriculture in the country was believed to lie in higher education and this resulted in the establishment of the Department of Agriculture and Technical Instruction. Some however feared the desire for Home Rule would diminish with a more contented population – by 'killing Home Rule with kindness'.

The Irish Parliamentary Party was finally reunited in 1900. Due to rivalries between the anti-Parnellites, John Redmond was chosen as the party's compromise leader. He lacked the authority of his predecessor, Parnell, but successfully led the IPP in the general election of that year. The 1902 Land Conference, with Redmond representing Ulster tenant farmers, resulted in the Land Act of 1903. This enabled tenants to purchase land, with the government paying the difference between the price offered by them and that demanded by landlords.

Both general elections in 1910 resulted in a hung parliament, with the Irish Parliamentary Party holding the balance of power at Westminster. Redmond now used his leverage to have the third Home Rule Bill introduced in 1912. This marked the pinnacle in his political career. The Ulster Unionists, however, campaigned persistently against the Bill. Edward Carson, who like Redmond had attended Trinity College and studied law, declared *'a united Ireland within the lifetime of any one now living would be out of the question.'*

The Ulster Volunteers, the unionist militia opposed to Home Rule, was formed in 1912 and its counterpart, the Irish Volunteers, was established the following year and led by Redmond. The battle lines were drawn between north and south with the spectre of civil war on the island.

In 1914, the Home Rule Act passed all stages in the House of Commons. But the Lords demanded that a clause be added that would temporarily exclude the Six Counties from Dublin rule for six years. Redmond and his party reluctantly agreed, saying *'Ulster will have to follow'*. The Act was passed in September 1914 but Home Rule was postponed for the duration of the First World War which had broken out two months earlier.

John Redmond initiated a fitting memorial to Charles Stewart Parnell. He chose the eminent Dublin-born sculptor Augustus Saint-Gaudens, who was raised in New York by his Irish mother and French father, to design the statue. The Parnell Committee was formed in 1898, the centenary of the 1798 Rising, to raise funding. Redmond successfully collected the finance for the project in America. The statue was cast in bronze six weeks before Saint-Gaudens' death in 1907. The committee proposed locating the monument opposite the old parliament building on College Green. This would have involved moving the statue of the bard Thomas Moore, the son of Wexfordwoman Anastasia Codd, to another location. Instead, Dublin Corporation instructed it to be located at the north end of Dublin's Sackville Street, bookending with the statue of O'Connell at the far end. Redmond performed the unveiling of the Parnell Monument on 1 October 1911. It was agreed that Great Britain Street be renamed Parnell Street on the same day. Nearby Rutland Square, where the Irish Volunteers' first public meeting was held in 1913 in the Rotunda Theatre, was changed to Parnell Square in 1933.

John Redmond proposed the erection of the iconic Parnell Monument on Sackville Street, Dublin.

Ulster Unionists promptly enlisted to support the British war effort at the outbreak of WWI in July 1914. Redmond called on all the people of Ireland, both north

John Redmond speaking outside the Tholsel building in the Bullring, Wexford, October 1914. (photo: Charles Vize)

and south, to support the war in Europe by enlisting. He calculated that nationalists and unionists fighting together for a common cause would unify them and believed that Home Rule, without the partition of the northeast, would be granted at the conclusion of the war. Redmond's decision split the Irish Volunteers, although the vast majority supported him.

Of the 142,000 members of the Volunteers, the more militant nationalists, numbering fewer than 10,000, were angered by Redmond's support for the war. The Redmond faction became known as the National Volunteers and on Easter Sunday 1915 held a rally of over 20,000 in the Phoenix Park in Dublin. But *'England's difficulty is Ireland's opportunity'* served as a rallying cry for the more militant Irish Volunteers, who launched the Easter Rising a year later. The week-long rebellion was a military failure and destroyed any possibility of a political settlement with the British.

Redmond's popularity diminished as the First World War dragged on. More than 30,000 Irishmen died, including over 870 from Wexford. John's own brother Willie was a casualty of the fighting in Flanders in 1917. He is remembered in Redmond Memorial Park in Wexford. With his own health failing, John Redmond died in London in March of the following year, aged 61. His funeral service was held in Westminster Cathedral and his remains were interred in the family vault in St John's Graveyard in Wexford town.

By the end of 1918 membership of the militant Volunteers had risen to about 100,000. In the general election of 1918, Sinn Féin overtook the Irish Parliamentary Party and independence was declared. The fourth Home Rule Bill of 1920 was never enacted. Instead, the Irish War of Independence resulted in the 1922 Anglo-Irish Treaty and the partition of Ireland.

Saga of the Famine ship they named *Dunbrody*

The busy timber-trading and shipbuilding port of Quebec in 1858, with 'Dunbrody' seen on the right.

'IT TOOK 115 YEARS to make this trip and 6,000 miles and three generations', declared the great-grandson of local man Patrick Kennedy on the New Ross quayside in 1963. Patrick had worked as a barrel-maker in the Creywell Brewery. *'Cherry's Ale for the Cheery Gael'*, ran the Cherry Brothers' advertising slogan. They established their Creywell Brewery in New Ross in 1830. This Kennedy was returning to County Wexford as the most powerful man on the planet.

The young trainee cooper embarked on *Dunbrody* in November 1848 and sailed to Liverpool. The city had been a staging post for hundreds of thousands of Irish emigrants fleeing the Famine in Ireland in the 1840s. From there, the majority of those who survived typhus, dysentery, cholera and hunger, took 'coffin ships' to North America. But when Kennedy came ashore, the numbers of Irish refugees arriving in Liverpool had already diminished. He remained in the city for four months before boarding the *Washington Irving,* bound for America. He arrived in Boston in April 1849 after four weeks at sea. His fiancée, Bridget Murphy from Gusserane, followed not long after and they married in Boston in September of the same year. Just three generations later, the future President of the United States was born to their grandson in 1917.

Dunbrody, named after the thirteenth-century abbey near Campile, was commissioned, along with seven sister ships, by William Graves & Son, timber merchants and shipping company in New Ross. They had a fleet of cargo vessels that transported wood from Canada to New Ross and other Irish and British ports. Their ships, numbering up to twenty, were also sent to every continent to trade in other commodities such as coal, cotton and iron.

William Graves (1787-1859) was born into a prominent Protestant family in Thomastown, County Kilkenny. He married Sarah Elly, daughter of Samuel Elly, a Quaker of New Ross. Their son, Samuel, born at Rosbercon Castle, who was educated at Scarview House, a private school in Taghmon, established his own highly successful shipping business in Liverpool in 1846. He became mayor of the city in 1860 and was elected MP for 1865-73. Samuel Graves named his home on the outskirts of Liverpool, Annefield House, after the townland next to Rosbercon Castle. As mayor, he proposed to develop some of his land for a football club and so Anfield Stadium was built in 1884 and is the landmark home of Liverpool Football Club. James, the youngest of their four sons, moved to Savannah, Georgia, where he set up another branch of the family's shipping empire in 1848.

William Graves engaged Thomas Oliver of Quebec to construct the 458-ton barque *Dunbrody*. Thomas Oliver, himself an immigrant from Derry, was an expert shipbuilder based in the great timber-trading city on the St Lawrence River. A dozen shipyards, scattered along the river bank, launched over a hundred vessels in one season. Edward Oliver, a brother of Thomas, moved from shipbuilding in Quebec to Liverpool, where he became a major shipping broker, specializing in selling Canadian-built ships to British operators. But according to the *Northern Times* in December 1854, he had a large inventory of sailing ships, which

Thomas Oliver, who built the original
'Dunbrody' in Quebec in 1845.
(Art Gallery of Ontario)

he anticipated chartering as Crimean War (1853-6) transports. However, the military chartered many steamships instead, forcing Edward Oliver to declare himself bankrupt.

Construction of the three-masted *Dunbrody* was supervised by John Baldwin and completed in six months. Baldwin would be her skipper for the first three years. New Ross native, 27-year-old John W. Williams, was her captain for the subsequent twenty years. She sailed out of Quebec bound for New Ross, Ireland's only inland port, carrying a cargo of timber on her maiden voyage in 1845.

Potato blight had already spread from South to North America in the previous year and was carried across the Atlantic to Europe in holds of cargo ships in 1845. The disease reached Ireland in August of that same year, leading to mass starvation, death and emigration over the next seven years. A quarter of the population, over two million people, left Ireland, mainly travelling to the USA and the British Province of Canada to start a new life.

Most of the ships that sailed to collect timber in the colony crossed the Atlantic without cargo. Now vessels such as *Dunbrody* were adapted to carry passengers on the outward journey, such was the demand for capacity during the Famine years. Bunks were added for the twice-yearly sailings, usually in April and September, from 1845 to 1851, avoiding the frozen winter conditions in Canada. The cities of Quebec and Montreal were only accessible during the summer season when the St Lawrence River was free of ice. Measuring six feet square, a single bunk was allocated to four adult passengers and their children. Conditions for steerage passengers, travelling in the cheapest accommodation, were tough. On other ships, as many as half of the passengers did not survive the arduous journey, already weak from hunger and disease before setting sail from Ireland. The mortality rate on *Dunbrody,* however, was extraordinarily low. On one voyage at the height of the Famine in 1847, *Dunbrody* carried 313 passengers, nearly

EMIGRATION
FROM NEW-ROSS FOR NEW-YORK.

THE favourite coppered and copper-fastened first-class Packet-Ship "DUNBRODY," JOHN WILLIAMS, Commander, is intended to sail from NEW-ROSS for
N E W - Y O R K
ON THE THIRD OF APRIL.
This superior Ship is too well known to require much remarks; she is famed alike for her Speed and Comfort as a Passenger Ship. She will be supplied with the usual quantities of Bread-Stuffs, Water, and Fuel, &c.
☞ To secure Cabin or Steerage Berths, early application is necessary to
WILLIAM GRAVES & SON.
New-Ross, March 14, 1849.
N.B.—The "Dunbrody's" destination is changed from Quebec to New-York—the "Aberfoyle" going to Quebec in lieu of "Dunbrody" 29th March : and another Ship is fixed to succeed the "Jane" for Quebec in place of the "Aberfoyle." The "Jane's" sailing day is the 10th of April.

Wexford Independent, 1849.

EMIGRATION FROM ROSS & WATERFORD TO QUEBEC.

THE following First-class remarkably fine Packet-Ships "DUNBRODY," "WARD CHIPMAN," and "GLENLYON," are intended to be despatched from ROSS and WATERFORD to QUEBEC, on the 12th, 18th, and 28th of APRIL.
These large and favourite Vesselsare well known as safe and regular Packet Ships, and as usual will be fitted and provisioned with particular care, for the health and comfort of Emigrants. Each Ship is to carry an experienced Surgeon.
Apply to the Owners, WILLIAM GRAVES and SON, New-Ross; or to their Agent, Mr. KYRAN DEA, Kilkenny.
P.S.—Owing to the great prosperity of Canada, the demand for labourers, &c., has greatly increased through the entire of that country—thousands are advertised for, at wages from 5s. to 7s. currency, per day. Emigrants bound to the State of New-York and Western portions of the United States, or of Canada, will find Quebec the cheapest landing port ; from the great extent of cheap inland water navigation up the St. Lawrence, and the vast Lakes of America.
February 20th, 1854.

Kilkenny Journal, 1854.

twice her normal complement, but only six perished. Indeed, her captains, Baldwin and Williams, both received much praise for their dedication, in letters from passengers writing home. John Williams wrote hundreds of letters from the ship to his employers back in New Ross. In one, following a stormy passage to Quebec, he wrote: *'The poor passengers were greatly frightened. They thought they should never see the land again.'* In 1847, when he was commander of another Graves ship, *Aberfoyle*, he created a hospital area on board and nursed sick passengers himself.

There were other reports of kindness shown to some emigrants who travelled on *Dunbrody*. The Gorey Workhouse recorded in 1855 that forty-three 'female paupers', most aged between 17 and 20, and nine children were selected to travel on *Dunbrody* to Quebec. We learn that each was to be provided with supplies for the journey, including *'30 pounds of salt meat or fish, vegetables consisting of potatoes, parsnips, carrots or turnips, bedding, saucepans, drinking vessel, knife, fork, plate and spoon'.* Leaving the workhouse, the house master gave each of them two pounds of white bread. *'On their arrival in Ross Mr Higginbotham (clerk) and Mr Thomas Harvey emigrant agent in Gorey had all their beds ready in the ship where they slept those nights. He had to give them their breakfast of bread and tea next morning as the cooking apparatus was not ready. They all expressed their gratitude in tears to the guardians for their kindness. Their conduct and appearance was the admiration of every person that saw them.'*

Dunbrody and other Graves-owned ships transported thousands to a new life in Quebec and New York. Many of the passengers were tenant farmers and their families who had worked on the vast estates of Lord Fitzwilliam in County Wicklow. Between 1847 and 1856, almost 6,000 poor tenants, unable to pay their rent, were offered paid passage and money to help them settle on the far side of the Atlantic.

An immigration station on the island of Grosse Île in the St Lawrence Estuary, on the approach to the French-speaking Catholic city of Quebec, was established

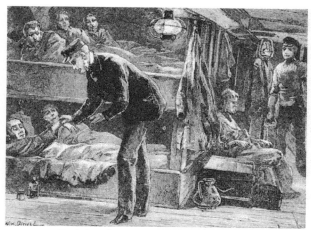
Depiction of a scene on a Famine ship en route to America.

in 1832. It was intended to contain a cholera epidemic believed to have been caused by European immigrants. The deserted station was reopened to quarantine Irish immigrants who had contracted typhus during their voyages from Ireland. In May 1847, the island was overwhelmed. By the end of the month forty ships formed a two-mile line down the St Lawrence River,

Inauguration in 1909 of the monument to the Irish immigrants who died during a typhus outbreak in 1847 on Grosse Île, Quebec.

all affected with the fever. Sometimes called Canada's Ellis Island, almost half a million Irish immigrants passed through Grosse Île when they arrived in Canada. Over 3,000 Irish people died in squalid conditions in fever sheds on the island. They were buried in the island cemetery along with another 2,000 who had perished en route from Ireland. This is the largest burial ground for refugees of the Famine outside Ireland. In 1909, a fifteen-metre tall Celtic cross memorial was unveiled on the highest point on the small island and is the largest of its kind in North America.

After 24 years of service, William Graves & Son sold *Dunbrody* in 1869. While en route from Cardiff to Quebec in 1874, her captain decided not to wait for the necessary assistance of a pilot to navigate the St Lawrence and she promptly ran aground. *Dunbrody* was bought by a salvage company that repaired her and sold her on to another shipping company. The following year, on her return sailing to Liverpool carrying a full cargo of timber valued at £12,000, she was blown off course in a fierce gale towards Canada's Labrador coast and again grounded. This time she was damaged beyond economical repair, abandoned and left to disintegrate.

THE REPLICA SHIP

Seán Reidy was 14 when President Kennedy visited New Ross and the original family homestead in Dunganstown. In 1991, the John F. Kennedy Trust, which was founded in New Ross three years earlier, was planning to open a heritage centre in the town to boost tourism. Seán was successful in securing the position of project manager. What impressed the trust most was his idea to build a full-size replica of *Dunbrody* that would be moored on the quayside to attract tourists.

A former employee of Graves, which had become a builders' providers until it closed in 1986, had in his possession old files from the shipping company going back to the 1840s and 50s. The archive, now held by the National Archives of Ireland in Dublin, contains letters of negotiation with agents, crew agreements, letters from prospective passengers, receipts for supplies and letters to Graves from its ships' captains. But most importantly, found among the treasure trove was the original bill of sale for *Dunbrody* with the precise dimensions of the ship.

With the endorsement of Senator Ted Kennedy and his sister, Jean Kennedy Smith, the US Ambassador to Ireland, the uphill task of fundraising for the estimated €3million to pay for the construction of the replica ship and interpretive centre was underway. The Ross Company Boatyard in New Ross, which had closed in the 1980s, was to be refurbished to construct the vessel. The renowned English naval architect Colin Mudie, who had worked on the replica *Matthew* in Bristol, was appointed to draft plans for *Dunbrody*, based on the design of the original.

Construction started in 1996 and over the course of five years apprentice

The Dunbrody Visitor Centre and replica 'Dunbrody' on the Barrow River, New Ross. (photo: Des Kiely)

The magnificent 'Dunbrody' in the International Tall Ships parade in Waterford in 2005. (photo: Paddy Donovan)

shipwrights, trainee carpenters and more than 150 local people gained hands-on experience in traditional shipbuilding skills. Oak was sourced in Wicklow for the ship's frames and the major structural timbers were brought from Africa. All the ironwork was produced on-site. There were over 100,000 visitors to the dry dock during construction. With the final outfitting and rigging completed, *Dunbrody* was launched in February 2001.

In 2005, she took part in the International Tall Ships event in Waterford. This was her maiden voyage. With *Asgard II* and *Jeanie Johnston*, she joined the tall ships fleet in the 'parade of sail'. The following year, *Dunbrody* sailed across the Irish Sea to Milford Haven in Wales. This was to mark the partnership that had been enjoyed with Pembrokeshire College, whereby students of boat building and design had worked on the construction of *Dunbrody* in New Ross. This was to be her final voyage. It was decided to have her permanently moored on the quayside for tourists.

A comprehensive database compiled directly from original ships' manifests is available on the website www.dunbrody.com The Irish Emigration Database records Irish immigrants arriving in New York between 1846-90. Arrivals in Boston, Baltimore, New Orleans and Philadelphia cover the Famine years 1846-51.

'Dunbrody' in the Tall Ships event in Waterford, 2005.

The Knights of Templetown and their Friday 13th downfall

The building complex at Templetown on the Hook Peninsula. The 12th century church of the Knights Templar stood to the left of the Norman tower, built by the Knights Hospitaller in the 14th century. On the right are the ruins of the Protestant church built in 1828 and closed in the 1930s. (photo: Des Kiely)

THE KNIGHTS TEMPLAR was an elite order of medieval knights created in the 12th century, forming part of the Crusades to win back the Holy Land from the Muslims. They were a very powerful and wealthy force in Christendom for almost 200 years. The knights created nearly a thousand strongholds across Europe and the Holy Land. Following the Anglo-Norman conquest of Ireland, King Henry II granted them land on the Hook Peninsula in an area since known as Templetown. But Philip IV of France had hundreds of members arrested and tortured in Paris and across Europe in October 1307, on Friday 13th. The date still strikes fear into people.

Probably the best documented link to the Templars in Ireland is at Templetown. From their tower house the knights protected access to the port of Waterford along the strategic promontory of Rinn Dubháin, later translated as Hook Head. In the church graveyard next to the tower house a rare example of a Knights Templar grave slab can be seen. Rectangular in shape, it bears the Templar symbol of a lamb and cross.

The order of the 'Poor Fellow-Soldiers of Christ and the Temple of Solomon' – later known simply as the Knights Templar – was created in 1118 in part to protect pilgrims travelling to the Kingdom of Jerusalem. Port cities such as Acre and Jaffa were then in Christian hands, as well as Jerusalem itself. But as they made their way overland to the holy city, hundreds of pilgrims were routinely slaughtered by Muslims. The monastic order of knights was based at the site of the Temple Mount in Jerusalem and it expanded rapidly. They received enormous financial donations to help their fight in the Holy Land and soon were no longer 'poor soldiers'. Pope Innocent II decreed in 1139 that members of the order were free from paying taxes and were answerable only to the authority of the Pope.

The heavily armoured Templar knights took part in key battles of the Crusades to recover the Holy Land from Islamic rule. The order also managed the assets of the many noblemen who enlisted, eventually making them financially powerful throughout the Christian world. They established strongholds at strategic locations across Europe and the Holy Land.

However, Henry II decreed that the Church was not above the law. This finally led to the murder of Thomas Becket, Archbishop of Canterbury. Becket, who continued to excommunicate royal servants, was murdered in 1170 by four of the king's knights, believing it to have been the wish of the king.

On 18 October 1171, Henry and his army landed at Crooke on the west shore of Waterford Harbour with a fleet of 400 ships. He was the first English monarch to set foot in Ireland. His purpose was to assert his position over the country and the recently arrived Anglo-Normans. The lands taken by the Norman invaders were to be handed over to the king and he set up a feudal system of government for the island. He had fortified castles constructed in the form of tower houses surrounded by strong walls to protect these new lands.

Having spent the winter in Dublin, Henry travelled to Wexford, where he is said to have done

The manor of Kilcloggan (greyed area) on the Hook Peninsula was granted to the Templars by Henry II in 1172.

This sketch from the 1800s by the Dublin artist and geologist George Du Noyer shows the ruins of the Templar church (left) that once stood at Templetown.

penance in Selskar Abbey. As part of his contrition for the death of Becket, Henry also vowed to provide for the upkeep of two hundred Templars. He issued a charter in 1172, granting extensive estates or 'vills' in Ireland to the Knights Templar. The vill of Clontarf in Dublin was to be their main administrative headquarters, with other lands granted from Louth to Sligo to Waterford as well as mills in Wexford town, probably on the Bishopswater stream. To protect shipping in Waterford Harbour, he assigned lands to the 'warrior monks' at Crooke on the western shore and Hook Peninsula on the eastern shore.

The manor of Kilcloggan comprised over 5,000 acres on the peninsula, from Hook Head to just south of Duncannon. The Knights Templar built their church overlooking a landing area now known as Templetown Bay. Their lands also included the ancient church of St Alloch and site of an early monastery at Kilcloggan (a corruption of *Cill Ealloch*, Church of Alloch in Irish). To the north were Cistercian lands on which Dunbrody Abbey would be built. In later years the Templars were embroiled in aggressive land disputes with their Cistercian neighbours.

Henry II spent seven weeks in Wexford town awaiting good weather before setting sail to Wales in April 1172. He was forced to embark from the outer harbour due to the sandbanks blocking the harbour entrance. He granted Wexford town to Richard de Clare ('Strongbow') the following year.

Outside the present-day Bride Street Church in Wexford town stands an altar with a plaque that reads: '*This altar was taken from the ruins of the Knights Templar Church, Kerlogue (1887) on St. Elloch's early foundation. The knights preceptory declined with the supp-*

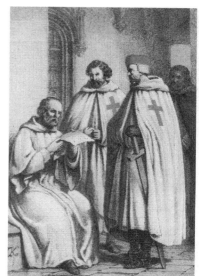

The Knights Templar warrior monks dressed in white habits bearing a red cross.

ression of the order (14th century). The altar was used again in Penal times (1650-1730)'

Not all of the knights who settled on the Hook were warriors. Many were likely elderly monks, involved in collecting rents from the order's estate.

A notable member was William Marshal, who joined a two-year Crusade to the Holy Land in 1183. He developed the town of New Ross between 1192 and 1207 and commissioned the construction of the Tower of Hook to protect shipping into the expanding trading port. When he knew he was dying in 1219, he was invested in the order of the Knights Templar. He was buried as a simple knight in a Templar robe in the Temple Church in London, the order's English headquarters.

DOWNFALL

Over nearly 200 years the Knights Templar had become the most dominant force in Christendom. As payment for protection, many royals and aristocrats donated large estates. They now owned vast swathes of property and were so wealthy that they were one of the most efficient and largest banking networks in medieval Europe. But this all changed in 1291 following the Siege of Acre, the capital of the Kingdom of Jerusalem. The Knights Templar were defeated at the port city and so the Holy Land was lost again to the Muslims. There was now no longer a need for the Templars, who returned to their various religious manors across Europe.

Many of the ruling classes blamed the Templars for the defeat. They were now accused of everything from heretic beliefs and rituals to spitting on the cross, sodomy, fraud and financial corruption. King Philip IV of France, who

The altar from the old Knights Templar foundation at Kerlogue outside Wexford town. It was moved in 1956 and reassembled where it now stands outside Bride Street Church.

was heavily in debt to the Templars and was in need of money to unite the various provinces of France, introduced a kingdom-wide tax. Pope Boniface VIII opposed his taxation plan and Philip, in retaliation, accused the Pope himself of heresy. In 1306, Philip expelled all Jews and Italian bankers from France and seized their assets. He then went after the Knights Templar, ordering their arrest, thereby challenging the authority of the new Pope, Clement V.

The coordinated arrests across France were carried out at dawn on Friday 13th October 1307. Templars were hauled from their beds and from prayer and thrown into prison. They were severely tortured before confessions were extracted from them. In 1310, fifty-four Templars were taken in carts to a field just outside Paris, where the horses were released and the carts set ablaze with the monks still inside. Pope Clement was finally forced into dissolving the order of the Knights Templar in 1312 and handed most of their property over to the rival Knights Hospitaller. Having spent seven years in jail, the Grand Master of the Knights Templar, Jacques de Molay, and three others were burned at the stake in 1314 in front of the yet to be completed Cathedral of Notre Dame in Paris.

In 1307, the newly-crowned king of England, Edward II, lost no time in backing Philip of France and ordered all lands and property belonging to the Knights Templar to be confiscated. Members of the order on the Hook Peninsula were imprisoned in Dublin Castle, with income from the manor of Kilcloggan, as well as Crooke and Kilbarry in County Waterford, assigned to pay for their upkeep. When the order was dissolved five years later, their lands were handed over to the Knights Hospitaller.

KNIGHTS HOSPITALLER

Strongbow had introduced the Knights Hospitaller to the county in about 1175. They too were a military order, founded in

Kilcloggan Castle, built c.15th century by the Knights Hospitaller as their manor headquarters. (photo: Des Kiely)

Jerusalem to provide care for sick and injured pilgrims to the Holy Land. They were granted the borough of Ferns and the income from a number of churches in Wexford town, including St Michael's. Only the graveyard of St Michael's located on Michael Street survives. The Knights Templar church of St John, on the corner of John Street and John's Gate Street, is believed to have become part of the Hospitaller centre of operations in the town following the dissolution of the Templars. They established the Hospital of St John here, just outside the town wall

The Knights Hospitaller were identified by their distinctive white eight-pointed cross on a black background.

near John's Gate. Founded by William Marshal, the church was closed after Henry VIII's Act of Suppression of 1534. In Samuel Lewis's *Topographical Dictionary of Ireland*, 1837, he stated that 'some remains of the old church still exist.' But today all that survives is the graveyard, which contains the Redmond family vault and the remains of John Redmond. The churches of St Bride (Bride Street church now stands on the site), St Patrick (in ruins, Patrick's Square) and St Mary (in ruins, Mary's Lane) were bestowed on the Hospitallers by William Marshal in 1210 and confirmed by Pope Innocent III.

The Hospitallers were also granted the strategic borough of Ballyhogue on the banks of the Slaney. It was 1326 before they took possession of the manor of Kilcloggan. Here they built Kilcloggan Castle and this became their manor headquarters. After Henry VIII proclaimed himself head of the Church in Ireland in 1536, the Cistercian abbeys of Tintern and Dunbrody as well as the manor of Kilcloggan, were dissolved. Tintern was granted to the Colcloughs, Dunbrody was plundered and Kilcloggan later transferred to the Loftus family.

In 1522, the Hospitallers were forced out of Rhodes and relocated to Malta in 1530 (in exchange for providing a single Maltese falcon annually to the King of Spain), and remained there until 1798. Now known as the Order of Malta, membership numbers over 13,000 worldwide. In Ireland, its Ambulance Corps, with 4,000 volunteers, provides transportation, first aid and community and elderly care services.

Brunel's railway plan was to bypass Wexford town

The great Victorian civil engineer Isambard Kingdom Brunel (second from right) pictured in 1858, the year before his death.

THE FIRST railroad built in Britain for steam locomotives was opened in 1825 in County Durham. This was the world's first public railway to use steam engines. County Carlow-born William Dargan, along with engineer Charles Vignoles, designed Ireland's first railway linking Dublin's Westland Row and Kingstown (Dún Laoghaire), which opened in 1834.

The harbour at Kingstown was built between 1816 and 1859 using thousands of tons of granite from Dalkey quarries two miles away. The stones were transported by means of a horse-drawn tramway. The Dublin-Kingstown line was extended to Dalkey in 1844, utilizing the old tramline. A newly-invented atmospheric propulsion system for the ascent to Dalkey was employed – the first commercial railway of this type in the world.

The great civil engineer Isambard Brunel, while on a visit to Dublin to see the new system in operation, expressed the desire of the proprietors of the Great Western Railway (GWR) to establish a new cross-channel steamship route to the south-east of Ireland. The construction of a railway link between

Dublin and Wexford would be part of the venture. Brunel had engineered the GWR's railway that opened in 1838, linking London with the West of England and Wales. His vision was to connect London with the West of Ireland by train and steamer. Under the Regulating the Gauge of Railways Act 1846, the track gauge for Ireland was set at 5'3" and for Great Britain at 4'8½".

In 1844 the *Wexford Independent* reported that Brunel had prepared plans for the GWR to extend the 8-mile-long Dublin to Dalkey line, in three stages, to a new harbour to be located 100 miles away. And so the Waterford, Wexford, Wicklow & Dublin Railway (WWW&DR) was incorporated in 1846. The first stage of the new railway route was to connect Kingstown with Bray, the second to serve Wicklow and the third was to run to 'a pier in the sea or on the shore of Greenore Bay, near the town and port of Wexford.' The new harbour was to be constructed at Ballygeary just north of Greenore Point. The route through County Wexford would run east along the Slaney and cross the river over a new bridge to be built at Cullentra, half a mile upriver from Ferrycarrig. The route would bypass Wexford town. (The current plan for the M11 motorway extension to Rosslare Harbour is to follow this route).

The Wexford writer Thomas Lacy was employed in the 1840s to assist the solicitor responsible for negotiating rights of way for the construction of the railway from Dublin to Wexford. He subsequently published the diary of his travels in the book '*Sights and Scenes from Our Fatherland*' in 1863.

DUBLIN–ROSSLARE HARBOUR

The contract for an extension to Bray was awarded to the Dublin & Kingstown Railway and William Dargan was appointed chief engineer. His vision was to make Bray the 'Brighton of Ireland'. Although the Great Famine of 1845-49 was to have a crippling effect on the country's finances, the seaside town was transformed from the time the service came into operation in 1854.

The next section would link Bray and Greystones. To avoid having to construct the railway around Bray Head on the seaward side, it was proposed to route it inland. But this would have meant running the track through the Earl of Meath's Kilruddery estate. To avoid this inconvenience, the Earl granted land to take the route around the headland to the railway company free of charge.

James Stopford, the Earl of Courtown, turned the sod on the first stretch of railway at Bray Head in 1848 and Brunel was the engineer appointed to the project. It included building three tunnels and four wooden trestle bridges. The scenic route running on the edge of Bray Head to Greystones was described as an engineering feat and one of the most dramatic train journeys in the world. It was completed in 1856. However, all the original viaducts and cliff sections have since been demolished due to rockfalls, landslides and erosion. Over the decades the line had to be moved inland a number of times and several new tunnels needed to be constructed. The high maintenance costs led it to become known as 'Brunel's Folly'. In 1867, the Enniscorthy to Dublin train derailed while crossing one of the timber bridges, killing two passengers. Brunel died in 1859 aged 53.

The Dublin & Wicklow Railway (D&WR) company had extended the route to Wicklow by 1855. In order to continue the line to Wexford, it was necessary to purchase land owned by Earl Fitzwilliam, whose home Coollattin House in Shillelagh stood on his vast Coollattin estate. The result of negotiations with the company was the construction of a 16-mile-long branch line from Woodenbridge to Shillelagh, which opened in 1865.

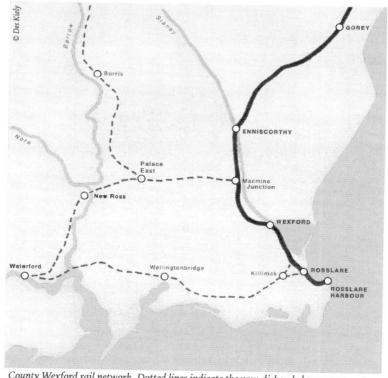

County Wexford rail network. Dotted lines indicate the now-disbanded passenger routes.

The line to Arklow and via Gorey and Ferns to Enniscorthy was completed by 1863. A new railway bridge was constructed over the Slaney to carry the railway southwards through a 405-yard tunnel that was dug beneath the town. The route from Enniscorthy continued along the west bank of the Slaney with a stop at Edermine Ferry (before the bridge was built) and Killurin, before it reached a temporary station near Carcur Bridge in 1872. The bridge had been built six years earlier to replace the old wooden Wexford Bridge linking the town with Ferrybank.

The banker, businessman and MP for Wexford, John Edward Redmond (1806-1865), grand-uncle of the later leader of the Irish Parliamentary Party, another John Redmond, had been behind the land reclamation south of Carcur, including what is now called Redmond Square. This enabled the line to be extended as far as Redmond Square, and Wexford Station opened in 1874. Redmond had earlier developed and extended the quay south from Paul Quay to the shipyard that he founded in 1832 (now known as Trinity Wharf).

Various plans were put forward to the Wexford Harbour Commissioners for the rail line along Wexford Quay. A solid quay wall was proposed as well as filling in the Crescent. Finally, the construction of a 20-foot-wide piled wharf was agreed. This was not without controversy, as reported in *The People* newspaper in 1877. The famous 'woodenworks' were a later addition and their dismantling was again controversial in 1996 when the rotting boardwalk was removed to facilitate the newly extended quayfront, completed in 2000. Meanwhile, the line connecting to the proposed new harbour at Ballygeary (Rosslare Harbour) faced many delays. The Crescent Bridge with its 40-foot opening span and the Coal Channel Viaduct on the South Slobs were two of the most important bridges to be completed. Cooper's cement and lime works in Drinagh were connected to the railway via a siding.

The railway from Dublin to Rosslare was finally completed in 1882 and included the erection of stations at Rosslare (Strand), Ballygeary and Rosslare Harbour. The service proved very popular, especially in summer, with seaside excursions running from Gorey on Sundays. In 1885, a second Wexford station was opened at White Wall (later known as the South Station) at the southern end of the town. But the Wexford-Rosslare Harbour line was unprofitable and closed in 1889 after just seven years.

Wexford Harbour had been in decline throughout the 19th century. George

A CIÉ diesel locomotive hauls a Dublin-Rosslare Harbour passenger service along Wexford Quay in 1975. The Guillemot Lightship museum was moored at the woodenworks from 1968 until 1986, when it was moved to Kilmore Quay and set in concrete. (photo: © The Carlisle Kid, cc-by-sa/2.0)

Bassett in his 1885 guide to Wexford described the harbour as: *'Treacherous but beautiful…the banks which obstruct its entrance shift so frequently as to render it difficult to accurately trace their movements'*. The pier at Rosslare that opened in 1882 was a 500-yard-long breakwater at this stage and not yet fit to accommodate large vessels.

ROSSLARE HARBOUR–WATERFORD

In 1856, a rail link was proposed from Waterford to Passage East and a ferry service or bridge to Ballyhack on the County Wexford side of the River Suir. A new railway would run via Duncormick to link with the DW&WR line at Carrig on the south bank of the River Slaney, close to Ferrycarrig, with a second branch to the new harbour to be built at Greenore. A company was formed, the Waterford & Wexford Railway (W&WR). A number of the local gentry were shareholders, including George Le Hunte of Altramont near Castlebridge, John Thomas Colclough of Tintern Abbey and Francis Leigh of Rosegarland near Wellingtonbridge.

Another thirteen years passed before the Rosslare Harbour Commission was established in 1869 to construct an 830-yard-long curved pier from the W&WR terminus. But nothing happened with the W&WR proposal and the planned rail link between Waterford and Wexford was abandoned.

The Fishguard & Rosslare Railways & Harbours Company (F&RR&HC) was created in 1894 to construct suitable ports at Fishguard and Rosslare and

The Barrow Bridge, the longest railway bridge in the country, on the Waterford-Rosslare line. (photo: Des Kiely)

a direct rail link between Rosslare Harbour, Waterford and Cork. The Wexford-Rosslare line reopened that year and work commenced on the extension of the pier at Rosslare Harbour. The engineer-in-charge of the harbour was Alfred Delap, who was married to Jane Jefferies of Newbay House, Wexford. His engineering firm Delap & Waller is still in business in Dublin today.

The Great Southern & Western Railway (GS&WR), formed in 1844, already linked Dublin with Limerick, Cork and Waterford. The Waterford to Rosslare Harbour route was begun as a joint venture with the F&RR&HC. Railway stations were built along the line at Campile, Ballycullane, Wellingtonbridge, Duncormick, Bridgetown and Killinick. The construction of the Barrow Bridge, the longest rail bridge entirely spanning water in Ireland, was carried out by Arrol of Glasgow. Construction began in 1902 and it opened in 1906. The bridge links County Kilkenny with Great Island on the County Wexford side of the River Barrow and two spans were pivoted to allow shipping to pass through, permitting access to New Ross.

The Dublin to Rosslare railway company went through many name changes, finally in 1906 settling on Dublin & South Eastern Railway (DSE). In Dublin it was nicknamed the 'Dublin Slow & Easy'.

Three steamships were commissioned to serve the Fishguard-Rosslare service and all three were launched in 1906. The *St. George* was built in Birkenhead and the *St. David* and *St. Patrick* at Clydebank. The official inauguration of the south Wexford line and Rosslare pier extension took place on 21 July 1906 and was performed by the Lord Lieutenant, Lord Aberdeen. With other dignitaries, he travelled from Dublin by train to Waterford and from there on the new line to Rosslare Harbour. The new port of Fishguard opened a month later. The Killinick to Rosslare Strand section came into use the following month, bringing the first train services from Cork to Rosslare Harbour. During World War One, 1914-18, the three 'Saints' were commandeered and used as hospital ships. They were replaced on the route for the duration of the war. The *St. Patrick* was badly damaged in a fire on arrival from Rosslare to Fishguard in 1929 and was substituted the following year with a new vessel, the *St. Patrick II*. The other two were replaced in 1932.

Rosslare Harbour in the early 1900s. The port was expanded through reclamation into the late 1990s. (photo: NLI)

MACMINE JUNCTION–WATERFORD

A rail connection between Dublin and Wexford via Carlow was proposed by the Bagenalstown and Wexford Railway in 1846. The first section from Bagenalstown to Borris opened in 1858 and was extended to Ballywilliam, County Wexford in 1862. This was the first railway station in County Wexford. An important feature of the Bagenalstown and Wexford Railway was the 16-arch viaduct at Borris. The line was further extended to Sparrowsland near Bree in 1870. A service by coach and horses between White's Hotel in Wexford operated to the train at Sparrowsland that brought passengers to Bagenalstown, where they changed to the GS&WR Kilkenny line to Dublin's Kingsbridge (Heuston) Station.

The last short section to Macmine Junction was finally completed in 1873. Here the line connected with the Dublin-Wexford line just north of Ballyhogue. But the Ballywilliam-Macmine route was underused and was sold two years later to the Dublin, Wicklow & Wexford Railway. They constructed a branch line from Palace East to Rosbercon, New Ross. This involved the construction of the red bridge across the Barrow and the Mount Elliott Tunnel in 1885. The line to New Ross opened in 1887. Work began on the New Ross-Waterford line in 1899 and it opened in 1904. Interestingly, the stations at either end were both located in County Kilkenny.

The Bagenalstown-Palace East and the Macmine Junction-New Ross lines shut in 1963. The New Ross-Waterford section is now disconnected but not officially shut. The derelict station at New Ross was demolished in 1997.

ACCIDENTS

County Wexford has witnessed four fatal train crashes; the first at Kilrane in 1907 when a locomotive collided with a passenger train, killing one person. The second accident occurred three years later at Felthouse Junction on the Wexford-Rosslare line when a goods train derailed and a fireman died. The junction closed later that year. Another person was killed when a locomotive crashed into a railway trolley in the Enniscorthy Tunnel in 1921.

Following a head-on collision of two passenger trains at Rosslare Strand

Scene of the fatal crash at Clogh near Gorey in 1975 that caused the death of five passengers. (photo: Irish Times)

Train derailed by the IRA at Ballyanne, Rathgarogue on the Palace East to New Ross line in 1923, during the Civil War.

station in 1974 that injured 15 people, the last and worst fatal crash in the county happened the following year on New Year's Eve, 1975. A large digger being transported on a low-loader accidentally collided with the underside of Cain Bridge on the Rosslare-Dublin line at Clogh, south of Gorey, knocking the railway tracks out of alignment and leaving them unsupported. The train travelling from Rosslare was derailed, causing the death of five passengers – two from Wexford town and one each from Ardcavan, Kilmore and Dublin.

CIVIL WAR ATTACKS

The signing of the Anglo-Irish Treaty in December 1921 led to the outbreak of the Civil War that lasted from June 1922 to May 1923. The IRA were split between anti- and pro-Treaty factions. The Wexford rail networks became the target of the South Eastern Division of the anti-Treaty IRA, whose aim was to disrupt the movement of the Free State Army in the region. One of their earliest attacks led to the closure of the Waterford-Rosslare route for the duration of the war. This was the blowing up in early July of the seven-arch Taylorstown viaduct near Wellingtonbridge. Other railway bridges were destroyed along the Waterford-New Ross line.

On 10 July 1922 an arched railway bridge near Killurin Station on the Wexford-Dublin line was damaged, causing the derailment of a goods train from Wexford. The attack was carried out by the 'Kyle flying column', a party of local Republicans commanded by Bob Lambert from nearby Kyle, Crossabeg. Two weeks later they ambushed the Wexford to Dublin train just after it emerged from the tunnel at Ferrycarrig, about 600 yards on the Wexford side of Killurin Station. News had reached Lambert's unit that the two coaches next to the engine were carrying an escort of 46 Free State soldiers and the third had 40 Republican prisoners, who had been recently rounded up around the county. They had blocked the line with railway sleepers, forcing the train to stop. From the wooded area above the track the IRA directed a hail of fire at the two coaches carrying the soldiers, killing two, with a third dying three days later from his wounds. Signal cabins were destroyed at Enniscorthy, Palace East and also at Macmine Junction, where the station was also burnt down. Further ambushes were carried out at Killurin with numerous trains, bridges and tracks destroyed on the county's rail network during the course of the conflict.

With the forced closure of the GS&WR Waterford-Rosslare line due to the destruction of the Taylorstown viaduct, the company announced it would cease operations in January 1923. This led to the Irish Free State passing the Railways Act 1924, forcing the amalgamation of the 'big four' railway companies and 22 smaller companies operating in the Free State. The GS&WR was by far the largest, with the Dublin-Cork mainline at its core. The Great Southern Railway Company was formed as a result. In 1945, the rail network became part of Córas Iompair Éireann, which was nationalized in 1950.

The GS&WR also operated a chain of hotels under the name Great Southern Hotels. The first was opened next to Killarney station in 1853. They opened other hotels around the country including one at Rosslare Harbour in 1969. Aer Rianta bought nine of the hotels from CIÉ in 1990 and they were later sold off separately to private investors around 2006.

The Waterford-Rosslare line remains the property of F&RR&HC, now jointly owned by Iarnród Éireann and Stena Line, and is the only mainline railway in the Republic not wholly owned by the State. The line closed to passenger traffic in 2010. A 24km cycling and walking greenway, following the old railway route linking New Ross with Waterford is underway. A similar greenway is planned from Rosslare Harbour to Waterford. The Dublin-Rosslare Europort route is now the only passenger train route servicing the county.

Wexford matron of post-war Hôpital Irlandais in Normandy

Saint-Lô in ruins in 1944 and inset: Mary Crowley, matron of the hospital set up in the town by the Irish Red Cross the following year.

THE TOWN of Saint-Lô lies on the banks of the river Vire on a route into the heart of France from the Normandy beaches. On D-Day, 6 June 1944 the Allies, who came to liberate France, began nightly bombings of the small market town, then in German hands, to delay the advance of their tanks towards the beaches. The Germans knew the importance of the town and realized if they could hold onto it, the Allies would be trapped. Saint-Lô was strategically positioned on a vital crossroads for the whole of Normandy and beyond, and its capture was pivotal to the Allied break-out across Europe.

After one week of relentless attacks, Saint-Lô, about the size of Enniscorthy, was reduced to rubble with 95% of its buildings destroyed and thousands of its inhabitants dead. An estimated 11,000 Allied troops and 3,000 Germans also lost their lives. The town would gain the unenviable distinction of having been the most heavily destroyed town in France in WWII and was given the name *Capitale des Ruines* (Capital of Ruins). When peace finally came a year later, help for the survivors who struggled to rebuild their lives arrived from neutral Ireland.

The Irish Red Cross assembled furniture, medical supplies and equipment to set up a 100-bed hospital to be shipped to Normandy along with doctors, nurses and support staff, including a store-keeper and interpreter from Dublin named Samuel Beckett. The matron of the hospital, Mary Crowley, hailed from Wexford town.

Mary Frances Crowley was the eldest of six children born to John Crowley and Emily (née Williams) who married in 1905 in Wexford. She was born the following year at 12 William Street, the home of her maternal grandparents, retired lighthouse keeper James Williams and his wife Margaret. Mary's father John was also a lighthouse keeper and at the time of her birth was stationed at Hook Lighthouse. John served on various lighthouses around Ireland, necessitating the family to move house frequently. Mary played a leading role in the household, supporting her mother in rearing her five younger siblings.

Now in her twenties, Mary moved to England to study nursing and remained for ten years to complete her studies while working in hospitals in Liverpool and London. She returned to Ireland in 1941 to join Sir Patrick Dun's Hospital, Dublin and later the Royal Victoria Eye and Ear Hospital, where she also served as assistant matron and nurse tutor.

The Irish Red Cross, established at the outbreak of World War II in 1939, began making plans in 1943 to send medical assistance to civilian casualties in Europe. Funds were collected through a temporary state lottery. When the guns at last fell silent in 1945, an advance party, including the prominent architect Michael Scott, soon travelled to Normandy and the almost-

The Irish Red Cross hospital in Saint-Lô comprised twenty-five white wooden huts constructed by the French Ministry of Reconstruction using local German prisoners of war.

Hospital staff standing beside an Irish Red Cross lorry outside the national stud farm at Saint-Lô where hospital supplies were stored. Samuel Beckett, interpreter, storeman and driver (standing third from left) and Col. T.J. McKinney, hospital director (second from right) with German POWs behind, September 1945. (photo: Irish Times)

obliterated town of Saint-Lô was chosen to build and run an Irish hospital. The town's municipal hospital and all of its pharmacies had been destroyed in the waves of American and British bombings. The Allies dropped leaflets on the town in advance of the attacks warning people to evacuate, but the papers were blown eastwards away from the town.

Mary Crowley was appointed matron to the new hospital and tasked with recruiting thirty nursing staff. She described transporting 'a complete hospital from one country to another' as a 'colossal task'. Mary prepared a list of the fundamental requirements: 200 beds and other furniture for both patients and staff, medical appliances, dressings, drugs, cooking utensils, food, etc. Red Cross volunteers made clothing, bedlinen and dressings and packed them for shipping at its emergency depot at Lincoln Place in Dublin. The Dublin Port & Docks Board made a warehouse available free of charge. The cargo included six ambulances, two lorries, electrical generators, 3,500 packages, food for six months, whiskey and half a million cigarettes (then scarce in France).

The most famous recruit was Samuel Beckett, who lived in France throughout the war, in his own words preferring 'France at war to Ireland at peace'. For a time he was a member of the Resistance, translating information and passing it on to British intelligence. He returned to Dublin after liberation to visit his family but, being a foreign national, was unable to go back to France. Beckett was recruited as storekeeper and interpreter for the Red Cross project and this facilitated his return to France. He took up the job a month before sailing to familiarize himself with the hospital cargo.

The Wexford Steamship Company supplied their cargo vessel *Menapia*, which they had specially equipped with cold storage to transport penicillin and blood serum. On 14 August 1945 the ship departed Dublin Port and arrived five days later at Cherbourg. There it was met by Colonel Thomas McKinney, director of the new hospital, and storeman Samuel Beckett, who had both travelled ahead. The 250 tons of supplies were unloaded onto railway wagons and taken to Saint-Lô by train. German prisoners of war transported the crates from the station to a vast national stud farm, about half a mile from the hospital. The badly-blitzed farm buildings were used as a storage facility.

The hospital buildings, consisting of ten single-storey wooden huts, were constructed on a sloping site previously divided into community allotments for growing vegetables. They were provided by the French Ministry of Reconstruction. About a thousand German soldiers, captured when the war ended, were being held in a nearby prisoner-of-war camp and some were used to construct the huts and paint them white inside and out. The prisoners also worked in the kitchen and as cleaners. An outpatients department was opened in early September and large numbers of patients were treated with penicillin – an antibiotic that had been unavailable locally until then. By October the pathology department was up and running and in the following spring baths were obtained from demolished apartments in Paris.

The wards were open for inpatients in December and the hospital now had six doctors, ten nurses and nine general staff. The matron, Mary Crowley, arrived on Christmas Eve. Samuel Beckett met her off her ship at Dieppe after a rough crossing. He drove 200 miles through snow, past landmines and over bailey bridges to reach Saint-Lô, just in time to hear midnight Mass in the town's roofless bombed-out cathedral. Choirs sang while snow fell magically down on the congregation inside. The first baby born in the hospital's maternity ward in January 1946 was named Patrick Noël. That same month saw the arrival of more nurses and medical staff as Beckett's five months as hospital storekeeper was coming to an end. He had found the work exhausting and was by now eager to return to Paris and his writing.

Matron Mary Crowley (far left) with staff at the Saint-Lô hospital.

L'hôpital Irlandais gained a reputation for its hospitality to anybody who stopped by. They even employed a 'house officer' to show curious visitors around the facility. Welcoming cups of tea were always on offer. The staff threw regular parties and were responsible for restarting dancing in the town. The hospital now had 25 huts including one for social events. St. Patrick's Day 1946 was celebrated with Irish songs, much appreciated by the locals who enjoyed the staff's *joie de vivre*.

The hospital was officially opened in April 1946 with Irish flags and garlands decorating the town. A parade through the rubble and dust of the ruined streets included representatives of both the French and Irish governments as well as local public figures. Music was provided by the band of the French Navy from Cherbourg, who played both countries' national anthems at a ceremony at the town's new war memorial, finishing with refreshments in the hospital's recreation hut.

By summer, the hospital was full to capacity with 115 beds occupied, a full complement of staff and an ambulance service that covered most of Normandy. The majority of the patients were local but some travelled from as far away as Rouen and Paris. Victims of exploding mines and crumbling buildings were regulary admitted to the 26 special surgical beds. The local population were living in temporary wooden housing as in other bombed towns throughout Europe. The mammoth task of rebuilding the town would involve about 3,000 workers and 2,000 prisoners of war.

The Polish Red Cross, impressed with the facility in Saint-Lô, asked the Irish branch to explore the possibility of setting up a similar hospital in Warsaw. Colonel McKinney and architect Michael Scott visited the city while personnel in the hospital back in Saint-Lô expressed an interest in moving to a new eastern-bloc site. But the project was abandoned because of too many difficulties with the new Soviet-imposed Polish government that was not recognized by Ireland. The transfer of staff from Saint-Lô to Warsaw was also seen as *'playing into the hands of Bolshevik propagandists. The…fact that they are from Catholic Ireland will be used as proof in Europe and America that the Polish authorities are not hostile to the Catholic Church',* according to the Irish diplomat Michael MacWhite following a visit to Iveagh House by a Father Collins, Assistant General of the African Missions.

The hospital was intended to run for about two years, so long as the Irish Red Cross was able to raise enough funds to maintain it. A date for handing over to the French had not been agreed. In the summer of 1946 the necessary funding from Ireland was running out and the hospital would soon have to be consigned to the French Red Cross. The mayor of Saint-Lô was informed in August that the Irish Red Cross would be leaving at the end of October. The town council said they regretted the decision and asked if they would reconsider. The mayor wrote to the Taoiseach, Éamon de Valera, to postpone the withdrawal. De Valera replied that the decision stood, enclosing a copy of a resolution from the local French medical union to the Irish Red Cross requesting them to immediately transfer the Irish hospital to French control. The hospital was providing free treatment and this was affecting the incomes of French doctors, some who had returned to Saint-Lô at the end of the war. The doctors claimed that patients who could afford to be treated in private clinics were being admitted. Two of the doctors who had requested the Irish to leave the hospital were also members of the town council but had not informed the mayor or council members of the resolution. Tensions erupted in what became known in local newspapers as the *affaire de l'hôpital irlandais.*

Demonstration by townspeople against the withdrawal of the Irish Red Cross from Saint-Lô, September 1946.

A protest march through the town was organized in which nearly 5,000 people took to the streets in appreciation of the Irish staff, asking them to continue the *hôpital irlandais* in its present form and demanding the resignation of the two doctors on the town council. The crowd marched to the hospital, where flowers were presented to the staff. A petition with more than 2,000 signatures was handed into the town hall. The mayor was mandated by the council to travel to Dublin to present the petition to the Irish government. Having met officials in Dublin, the mayor returned to say he was informed that the Irish Red Cross could not finance the running of the hospital for an extended time but agreed to stay an extra two months until the end of the year. The two doctors in question finally tendered their resignations from the council but the row continued to dominate the local press for weeks.

During the last two months of 1946, Irish staff were replaced by French and a smooth transition was achieved. Mary Crowley was replaced by a French matron and the first group of Irish nurses departed in early December. The mayor paid tribute to the Irish women and thanked them for their magnificent work, dedication and help to the small French town left in ruins. He said they would never be forgotten by the people of the town and the more than 1,400 patients who had received treatment. A farewell banquet was held a week before Christmas for all the staff, and the mayor conferred Colonel McKinney with the title of honorary citizen of Saint-Lô. On 2 January 1947, several hundred townspeople gathered at the train station to bid farewell to the last of the Irish staff. They were presented with flowers and many wept as they watched them leave.

The hospital remained under French management for another ten years and continued to be called *l'hôpital irlandais*. A brand new hospital building at the other end of the town opened in 1956, funded by American aid. Colonel McKinney was invited to attend the opening. The 'temporary' wooden huts were finally taken down and a school now stands on the site, with one of the huts still in use for indoor sports.

Mary Frances Crowley and her staff were awarded the *Medaille de la Reconnaissance Française* (Medal of French Gratitude). Mary, who never married, returned to her post in the Royal Victoria Eye and Ear Hospital, where she founded the Nursing Training School and became Director of Nursing Studies. She was a visionary with a determination to raise the standard of education for nurses and set them on a path to personal development. She changed the face of nursing in Ireland for the betterment of the patient. In 1974, Mary established a Faculty of Nursing at the Royal College of Surgeons, the first of its kind in Ireland or Britain and a rarity worldwide. Writing about the *hôpital irlandais* in 1987, Samuel Beckett said of Mary that her 'impressive matronage was essential to the success of this great enterprise.' Mary Crowley died in 1990. Beckett was awarded the *Médaille de la Résistance* from the French government and he married his French lover, Suzanne Dechevaux-Dumesnil, in 1961. He was awarded the Nobel Prize in Literature in 1969 and died in 1989.

Dean Mary Frances Crowley, founder of the nursing faculty in the Royal College of Surgeons in Ireland in 1974, the first of its kind in Ireland or Britain.

The pathology department at the Irish hospital in Saint-Lô had been set up and run by Dr. James Gaffney, a well-known Dublin pathologist. On his return to Ireland in September 1946 he took up an academic post in Trinity College. Returning from a meeting in Cambridge, where he had read a paper on pathology, he was killed in the first fatal crash of an Aer Lingus plane, in January 1952. The Douglas DC-3 (an ex-military Dakota) flying from London to Dublin, crashed in a blinding rainstorm in Snowdonia, North Wales killing all 23 on board. The worst Aer Lingus crash occurred sixteen years later when Flight EI 712 crashed near Tuskar Rock on a flight from Cork to Bristol in 1968, killing all 61 people on board including four crew. (That tragedy is comprehensively covered in *Fascinating Wexford History, Volume One*).

On the 50th anniversary of the establishment of the Irish Red Cross Hospital, the 'Seanaghy Saint-Lô' association was formed in the town to promote Irish culture. With the name derived from the Irish word for storyteller, *seanchaí*, they hold music and dance workshops and other activities. This extract from a poem by Beckett is engraved in the Saint-Lô library walls:

> *SAINT-LÔ*
> *Vire will wind in other shadows*
> *unborn through the bright ways tremble*
> *and the old mind ghost-forsaken*
> *sink into its havoc* – Samuel Beckett, 1946

Last public execution in Ireland was for Rathgarogue murder

The teachers' house (extended in the 1920s), where the murder victim Michael Fitzhenry lived, stands next to Rathgarogue Church. (photo: Des Kiely)

PRIMARY SCHOOL principal Michael Fitzhenry was bludgeoned to death in a drunken attack by his wife's cousin in 1863 at Rathgarogue, about five miles northeast of New Ross. His killer, Joseph Kelly, later claimed that Fitzhenry had refused to pay his father's passage to America. Kelly was hanged before a large crowd gathered on the green in front of Wexford Jail. This was the last public hanging in Ireland.

Ballyanne Poor School, the first school in the area, was erected in about 1795 on the Ballyanne demesne at Rathgarogue, situated at a crossroads on the Old Ross to Ballywilliam road. The one-room school was founded by Henry Houghton 'for the education of the poor' – both Catholic and Protestant. In 1833, Father John Rickard of Rathgarogue applied to the newly-established National Education Board for the building of a national school in the chapel yard. A house that could accommodate the teacher already stood on the site. However, the board objected to the location being 'on chapel yard ground'. A second site nearby, not connected to a religious institution, was suggested and approved. The new two-room school for boys and girls was built the following year.

Michael Fitzhenry, from the townland of Monamolin near Rathnure, began his career as an untrained teacher in nearby Templeudigan in 1855 when he was twenty years of age. Nonetheless, he was appointed principal of Rathgarogue boys' school in 1857 on the same day that Mary Roche was appointed principal of the girls' school. The following year Michael and Mary got married and took up residence in the teachers' house next to the new Rathgarogue Church, built the previous year. They had three children over the next five years.

Mary's first cousin Joseph Kelly lived four miles away in Poulpeasty in the direction of Enniscorthy. The village was located on the estate of Lord Carew of Castleboro House. Joseph and his wife Catherine lived with his 70-year-old father John on a 20-acre farm, which they rented from Lord Carew. The Kellys struggled to meet their debts and were one year in arrears with their rent. Joseph and Catherine were planning to emigrate to America. They asked Michael and Mary Fitzhenry to take over the farm, which they agreed to on the payment of £75. The landlord consented to this arrangement. An initial cash payment of £30 was to be handed over and the balance would clear their debts. It was also agreed that the father, John Kelly, would remain living in the farmhouse. The Fitzhenrys took control of the Poulpeasty farm in March 1863 but remained living in Rathgarogue. They had crops sown on their newly-acquired farm and also moved two of their children to live in the farmhouse, where three domestic servants were employed. Mary was pregnant with their third child.

Quay Street, New Ross, where Michael Fitzhenry, accompanied by Joseph Kelly, enquired from William Forristal, shipping agent, about passage to America in 1863. (photo: NLI)

On the evening of Friday 15 May, Michael and Mary Fitzhenry were on a visit to the Kelly farm in Poulpeasty to see their children. The father, John Kelly, said he had changed his mind about remaining on the farm and wanted to move to America with his son Joseph. Michael was asked by Joseph if he would pay his father's £6 fare, but he refused. After much arguing, Joseph demanded eight shillings that he was owed, which Michael promised to pay him the following day.

The killer and victim were drinking together in Lawless's public house (now Mannion's), beside the entrance (left) to Woodville House at Mount Elliott outside New Ross. (photo: Des Kiely)

The next morning, Michael Fitzhenry travelled into New Ross by donkey and cart from Rathgarogue to buy coal and provisions. He had about two pounds and ten shillings with him. After leaving, Joseph Kelly called again to Mary Fitzhenry and complained that his father was very upset that he was not being given the fare to travel to America. He became abusive and demanded the money. Mary asked a neighbour, Thomas Kinsella, who was going to New Ross, to find her husband and tell him pay the fare. Later that day, Joseph met up with Michael Fitzhenry in New Ross and together called to William Forristal on Quay Street (described in Lewis's *Topographical Dictionary of Ireland*, 1837, as an 'emigration agent, grocer and spirit dealer'). Michael had a £1 note changed and paid Joseph the eight shillings he was owed. They then enquired about obtaining emigration papers for the Kellys. William Forristal expressed doubt about John Kelly being able to travel, considering his age, but agreed to make out the papers and the agent accepted Fitzhenry's guarantee to pay at a later date, as neither he nor Kelly had enough money.

Joseph Kelly collected two lengths of iron, and Michael Fitzhenry, who had been drinking heavily in the town, bought fuel from Kehoe's coal merchants. They were spotted later that evening heading out of town together. The pair stopped at Lawless's public house at Mount Elliott, where they stayed until closing time at 10 o'clock. They left with another man, Patrick Kelly (no relation) from Ballinaberney. Fitzhenry was barely able to walk and was falling into ditches as they made their way to Ballywilliam three miles away, arriving around midnight. There they met Michael's father, Patrick Fitzhenry, who reprimanded his son about the condition he was in. Michael and Joseph then continued on the road to Rathgarogue. It was now the early hours of Sunday morning.

At around 7.30 that morning, Philip Murray was making his way the short distance from Ballycoheir to Mass in Rathgarogue when he came upon the bloodied corpse of Michael Fitzhenry. It was lying in a laneway a short distance from the church and appeared to have been dragged about ten yards off the road. Father Alex Kinsella was notified and he arranged that the RIC in New Ross be notified. A murder investigation began when police constables arrived from Ballywilliam, Ballinaboola, Carnagh and New Ross. No money was found on the body and the deceased's watch and black necktie were missing. Later that evening they arrested Joseph Kelly and his wife Catherine in Poulpeasty, but she was later released. The police searched their home and found an iron bar in the kitchen – the possible murder weapon.

An inquest was held in Michael Fitzhenry's own school in Rathgarogue the next day. It was attended by the coroner, five magistrates, three doctors and three senior police officers. A large number of people from the locality gathered and a 16-man jury was selected. The jury was shown the body and they attended the post-mortem. They also visited the murder scene. The inquest was adjourned at 8 o'clock that evening.

Dr. Howlett gave evidence the next day when the inquest resumed at one o'clock. He told the jury that he believed death was caused by blows to the head and body using a blunt instrument such as an iron bar. Witness Patrick Kelly said he believed that, as the three walked to Ballywilliam that night, Joseph was concealing a couple of iron bars under his coat. When the inquest ended in the early hours of Wednesday morning, the jury concluded that Michael Fitzhenry died from wounds to the skull and torso and returned a verdict of wilful murder against Joseph Kelly.

In a subsequent search around the Kelly home three days later, the second iron bar and black necktie were discovered concealed in a nearby ditch.

Kelly's murder trial opened in Wexford Courthouse on the quay opposite Wexford Bridge on 10 July 1863, with Baron Hughes presiding. Joseph Kelly pleaded not guilty. But the same witnesses who had given evidence at the inquest two months earlier repeated their testimonies, although none had witnessed the murder. The circumstantial evidence against the witness was so strong that it took the jury only eleven minutes to return a verdict of guilty when the trial concluded after two days. The judge put on the black cap and stated: *"...you Joseph Kelly, the prisoner at the bar, shall be taken from the place where you now stand to the place from whence you came, and there, at the usual place of execution, on Monday, 11th August, 1863, be hanged by the neck till you are dead..."* Kelly protested his innocence, eventually collapsing. It was nearly three quarters of an hour before he could be removed from the dock.

It was later noticed that the date of execution was a Tuesday and not Monday and so Joseph Kelly had to return to court at 5 o'clock to be sentenced again. The prisoner had to be forcibly removed from the dock and returned to Wexford Jail on Spawell Road.

The following Saturday's *People* newspaper led with an editorial on the death sentence passed on Kelly and pleaded with its readers not to attend the hanging. *"Will they come to see the terrible wrenching of soul from body, as they would go to a race or a cock-fight? Will they stand by when the Angel of Death is throttling his victim, and talk with unfeeling interest about the thickness of the rope, the height of the fall, the identity of the hangman, and all the other materials of savage gossip?"*

From the time sentence of death was passed until the day of his execution, the prison chaplain, Rev. James Roche, his assistants Rev. Thomas Clooney

The picturesque Rathgarogue railway station, which stood on the Palace East to New Ross extension of the Ballywilliam to Macmine line, was constructed by the Dublin, Wicklow & Wexford Railway. The route opened in 1887 and was closed in 1963.

and Rev. John Roice took turns to be continuously with Kelly in his cell each day to prepare him spiritually. Father Roche was the parish priest behind the building of the twin churches, completed five years earlier in 1858.

On the night before going to the gallows, Joseph Kelly handed a confession, witnessed by the prison clerk and turnkey, to Father Roice. It stated that at first he had not intended to kill Fitzhenry but only to give him a beating. After leaving him injured on the roadside he knew Fitzhenry would report him to the police and so returned and finished him off. *'I am heartily sorry for this horrible crime, and all the scandal I have given'*, he wrote.

The next morning a force of about 160 police constables formed a quadrangle around the scaffold erected on the green in front of Wexford Jail. Father Roche said Mass that morning in the prison and heard Kelly's confession twice. The clergy had appealed to people not to attend the spectacle but an estimated 500 spectators turned up. *'It is a happiness to have to state that few respectable people attended, and that those who were present, though belonging to the low order of society, were most orderly in their conduct'*, reported *The People* newspaper. Father Roche accompanied Joseph Kelly to the gallows at 8am and requested the crowd to kneel and pray. *'The crowd then knelt, a considerable number, however, remained standing, who were probably persons professing the Protestant religion'*, suggested the paper. *'He was uttering "Jesus, Mary and Joseph"...and the unfortunate man launched into eternity. The unhappy felon yielded the ghost without a struggle'*, *The People* concluded. Three members of the constabulary and some in the crowd fainted.

Joseph Kelly's execution was the last public hanging carried out in Ireland. Five years later the Capital Punishment Amendment Act came into effect on 29 May 1868, putting an end to public executions. The passing of the Act followed campaigns by former Prime Minister Robert Peel and Charles Dickens, who both called for an end to the 'grotesque spectacle' of public hangings. The act required that in future executions were to be carried out within prison walls. The last public execution in the United Kingdom was carried out three days before the Act became law, when the Irish Republican Brotherhood member Michael Barrett was hanged in front of Newgate Prison in London on 26 May 1868. A crowd of 2,000 booed, jeered and sang 'Rule Britannia' as his body dropped.

Hundreds of foundry workers locked out for six months

Almost 400 workers were locked out of Pierce's, the largest of Wexford's three foundries. They operated at this vast site for 155 years, from 1847 to 2002. (photo courtesy John Hayes)

LABOUR UNREST in Wexford and the town's three foundries' refusal to recognize union membership resulted in about 700 of their workers being locked out for six months, between August 1911 and February 1912. Until then, this was the biggest lockout in the country, only surpassed by the most severe industrial dispute in Irish history a year later – the Dublin Lockout of 1913. Families struggled to survive as police baton charges broke out, resulting in the death of an innocent bystander. When a settlement was finally reached, bonfires and tar-barrels were lit on the streets and a jubilant crowd of 5,000 was addressed by James Connolly in the Faythe.

Until the 1880s, particular trades were organized into trade unions to protect their workers through mutual insurance, but strikes were rare. It was 1906 before the unions were given legal protection to conduct disputes. The Liverpool trade unionist Jim Larkin arrived in Belfast the following year. He organized dock workers into a union and called on them to strike for better wages. A year later he moved south to organize workers in Dublin, Cork and Waterford and founded the Irish Transport and General Workers' Union (ITGWU) at the end of 1908.

James Connolly, organizer of the ITGWU in Belfast and supporter of the Wexford strikers in 1911.

The Scottish socialist James Connolly and his Irish-born wife Lillie settled in Dublin. He joined what became the Irish Socialist Republican Party. They moved, out of economic necessity, to the United States in 1903 and when they returned to Ireland in 1910, Connolly became Larkin's right-hand man in the ITGWU.

The union was all-embracing, representing both skilled and unskilled workers. In June 1911, Larkin launched *The Irish Worker* newspaper, an alternative to the capitalist-owned local press. The paper carried coverage of the union's activities and denounced unfair employers; its circulation grew rapidly. The ITGWU opened an office on Charlotte Street in Wexford in the same month and working men promptly attended to sign up for membership.

The vast majority of labourers in Ireland had no vote in national elections until the Reform Act of 1918, when all men over 21 and most women over 30 would be given the vote. Redmond's Irish Parliamentary Party had done little to improve the conditions of workers and their families in Wexford. Membership of the new ITGWU was now seen as an opportunity for representation and fraternity among the town's tradesmen and labourers.

The town's employers, however, feared control might transfer to the union, thereby challenging the bosses' authority over their workers. They believed that Larkin had to be stopped and his union destroyed and it was the town's foundries that were first to take action.

Jim Larkin, c.1910. In 1908 he founded the ITGWU that exists today as SIPTU.

THE FOUNDRIES

The biggest employer was Pierce Ironworks. Kilmore-born James Pierce opened a small foundry on Allen Street in 1839 and moved to the Mill Road site eight years later. Pierce's developed into a thriving agricultural machinery business, exporting to Britain, Europe, America and Australia. There was a brief strike at the works in 1889 when the workforce numbered 140.

Management had attempted to place unskilled workers in positions held by fitters and turners. This resulted in the formation of the Wexford Fitters & Turners Society within the foundry. James's sons Philip, Martin and John succeeded him and in 1911 the business was in the hands of his surviving son, John. By 1914 Pierce's had 1,000 employees, making it the largest engineering or agricultural machinery manufacturer in the country.

Matthew Doyle from Ballygarrett established a forge in the 1850s, opposite where the Redmond monument would be erected in 1867, in Wexford town (the site is now occupied by Dunnes Stores). He had help from time to time from James Pierce and in 1880 set up his own foundry on the three-acre site with his sons William and Andrew. The business, Selskar Ironworks, flourished. Adjacent to the works, Matthew had three double-fronted houses, Auburn Terrace, built for himself and his two sons in 1891.

Star Ironworks of Cappoquin, County Waterford established the third farm machinery business in Wexford in 1897. It was located on a reclaimed site formerly occupied by Wexford Dockyard, constructed for John E. Redmond (grand-uncle of the Irish Parliamentary Party leader) in the 1820s. The Star was purchased in 1908 by the Hearn family of New Ross and became known as the Wexford Engineering Company. By 1911 it had more than 130 in its workforce. Having later housed Smiths Engineering, Wexford Electronix and Clover Meats, the site has long been cleared for future development.

Star Ironworks (Wexford Engineering) was located off Trinity Street, on the old Wexford Dockyard site.

THE LOCKOUT

The reaction of the foundries to their workers joining the ITGWU was swift. Doyle's Selskar Ironworks, the smallest of the three foundries, were the first to lock their men out on Monday 10 August 1911. A week later, Pierce's dismissed any worker who had joined the union. The ITGWU retaliated by blocking a shipment of coke destined for their furnaces. Pierce's responded by giving the remainder of their workforce of 400 one week's notice. A fortnight later, John Hearn of Wexford Engineering locked out nearly 200 workers on 29 August. 'No workman is acceptable if a member of the ITGWU,' said Hearn bluntly. ITGWU men were also barred from Thompson Brothers on Custom House Quay and Spawell Flour Mill (owned by the Mayor, Howard Rowe), located on Spawell Road where Redmond Park now stands.

There were now almost 700 foundry men out of work and over 3,000 men, women and children were now directly impacted by the lockout. The men had no alternative source of income and could only survive without wages for a short time.

P.T. Daly, the ITGWU organizer sent to Wexford.

Secretary of the Irish Trades Union Congress, Dubliner P.T. Daly, was appointed as an organizer within the ITGWU. Daly was a member of James Connolly's Socialist Party of Ireland and a highly experienced trade unionist. He was dispatched to Wexford on 21 August and negotiations soon got underway. Representing the workers on a conciliation committee were: P.T. Daly, Nicholas Lacy (Pierce's), James Underwood (Selskar) and Richard Corish (Star). On the other side were Howard Rowe, Father Hore, Archdeacon J.K. Lathen (St Iberius) and Aldermen James Sinnott, Robert Hanton and George Hadden (Snr). The committee submitted a set of proposals to both sides, whereby the workers could either join separate craft unions or a local union. But the ITGWU would not be recognized in the settlement.

Wednesday 6 September saw the arrival of a large contingent of RIC reinforcements in Wexford. Crowds anticipated their arrival at 7pm on the train from Dublin. When the policemen, numbering about 150, stepped onto the platform of the North Station, they were greeted with hoots and shouts from locals. The RIC men marched along the quays towards Barrack Street, followed by the large crowd that was heckling and began throwing stones. The police responded by baton-charging the crowd. At Allen Street and Gibson's Lane (Peter Street) they were confronted again by yet another crowd. Another baton charge that followed led to many injuries.

Those who sustained severe head injuries were treated in the County Infirmary on Hill Street and twenty civilians were kept in overnight. Among them were: Stephen Sinnott, John Harpur and Stephen Colfer (all from King Street), Thomas Callaghan, Laurence Walsh and John Boyt (all from Bride Street), James Lacey (High Street), Nicholas Redmond (Mary Street) and William Birney (Distillery Road). Patrick O'Connor had to undergo a life-saving operation for a fractured skull. James Bolger's injuries were so severe that he was unable to make the journey to the Infirmary and had to be treated at home by Dr David Hadden. Peter O'Connor from the ITGWU intervened and convinced the crowd to go home.

There were more disturbances between workers and the RIC on the streets of the town the following night. In one incident an innocent victim was 58-year-old Michael O'Leary. He had returned from work as a corn porter in Castlebridge and dropped into a shop to buy tobacco when he got caught up in a baton charge on Bride Street. O'Leary suffered severe head wounds and died some days later from septic meningitis. An 8-year-old boy, Thomas Whitney, was also struck on the head. *The People* newspaper described O'Leary as 'a respectable working man, of quiet and unobtrusive habit.' His funeral, led by St Brigid's Fife and Drum Band, was one of the largest seen in the town for many years.

Jim Larkin arrived in Wexford and addressed a mass meeting in the Faythe on 9 September. He vigorously rejected the proposal put forward by the conciliation committee and cited, among other things, the pitfalls of all the workers being members of small local unions that would inevitably be poorly funded. He said the workers would always be vulnerable to pressure from the big foundries, as was now the case during the lockout, and pressed for the obvious advantages of membership of the larger national ITGWU. Efforts to restart negotiations in late September failed because the foundry owners refused to meet if P.T. Daly was present.

In October, the foundries announced that they would be reopening and planned to use 'blackleg' labour. Some foundry workshops were converted into barrack-like accommodation. Pierce's offered a property they acquired –

Doyle's Selskar Ironworks was located in Redmond Place. The area was redeveloped in the early 1990s and is now known as Redmond Square. The site was later occupied by Meyler's Garage and now by Dunnes Stores.
(photo: Irish Agricultural Museum)

Brien & Keating's hardware (now part of Boot's) on South Main Street – which they had converted into a hostel. Newspaper advertisements were placed to recruit the strike-breakers, offering higher wages than were paid to local skilled tradesmen. Father Hore stated in a church sermon that these workers would 'not be of a high moral standard.' The blacklegs were brought in from Carlow and Dublin as well as England and Scotland.

The press were mixed in their reporting of the Wexford lockout. Arthur Griffith, through his newspaper *Sinn Féin*, was a consistent opponent of the ITGWU and advocated the use of the army to move goods blocked by the strikers. *The Free Press* also opposed the union, having initially supported the workers. Larkin declared that *The People* 'gave both sides a fair hearing'.

At another public meeting in the Faythe attended by 4,000 people, P. T. Daly publicly accused the *Wexford Record* editor, John Belton, of offering him £1,000 to withdraw himself and his union from Wexford. Belton lived above his bicycle shop on Common Quay Street. In a follow-up incident, as Daly walked down Monck Street to his accommodation in Morris's Hotel, he was attacked by Belton, who beat him over the head with a stick. The Infirmary refused to treat Daly's injuries and the RIC rejected his pleas to arrest Belton. Daly pressed charges of grievous bodily harm and at a subsequent court appearance, Belton was fined £1. It emerged in court that Belton was acting as an intermediary for Pierce's and was authorized to offer the workers an increase of four shillings per week if they abandoned the union.

There were many arrests for intimidation. Blacklegs were regularly attacked as they headed home after their day's work in the foundries. Middle management suffered regular attacks too and some had windows in their houses smashed. Richard Corish of William Street, an employee of the Star Ironworks, was a union organizer during the lockout. He was accused of 'following' men who continued to work rather than join the union and was detained overnight in the police barracks.

Richard Corish worked at the Star Ironworks before the lockout. He was blacklisted by them and never got his job back.

Hundreds of families were desperate as they faced into a bleak winter. Many workers left Wexford seeking employment elsewhere and some never returned. The ITGWU supported the strikers and Richard Corish actively fundraised for them. Local shopkeepers extended credit to hundreds of families. In October 1911, the Workers' Aid Committee held a fundraising variety concert in the Theatre Royal, Wexford which was full to capacity. At the interval, P. T. Daly thanked the audience on behalf of the strikers. James Connolly addressed a rally in Belfast and sought support for the locked-out workers. Donations also arrived from Dublin, Cork and Britain. The GAA organized games to fund the men and their families. They held parades carrying black flags but these ended with clashes with the police. The entire proceeds from the Leinster Senior Hurling Championship of 1911, between Kilkenny and Dublin, were donated to the fund. The game was played in Portlaoise, with Kilkenny winning 4-06 to Dublin's 3-01.

On 8 January 1912 in Rowe Street Church, as the Boys Confraternity, under the supervision of Father Wickham, was about to get underway at 8pm, the teenagers were joined by John Gregory, a nephew of the owners of Selskar Ironworks. The boys objected to his presence and called for his removal but Gregory refused to leave. A number of them left in protest and chanted and sang outside the church, where they were soon joined by a large crowd. According to *The People*, they 'shouted in the side doors of the church and interrupted the recitation of the Rosary.' Father Wickham denounced the protesters and said Gregory was most welcome. A large squad of RIC arrived on the scene and at the end of the service escorted the young boy home.

When P.T. Daly returned to Wexford in mid-January after a short absence, he was greeted at the North Station by a large enthusiastic group that escorted him to his hotel. He addressed yet another public meeting in the Faythe on 23 January, at which he called for the establishment of a 'workers police force'. A few days later, Daly was arrested as he sat in the ITGWU office on Charlotte Street and taken to George's Street Barracks. There he was charged with incitement and hastily brought before a magistrate. He was duly sentenced to three months detention in Waterford Jail and refused bail. Hundreds of supporters cheered along the route, waving hats and handkerchiefs, as he was driven the short distance to the North Station and put on a train for Waterford.

THE SETTLEMENT

Daly, who had maintained the dispute for four months, had now departed and the situation for the striking men remained grim. Intimidation of the blacklegs was a daily occurrence. Many of them, particularly those from England, were feeling uncomfortable about having taken the mens' jobs and depriving them of their incomes, and so some began to leave.

Jim Larkin instructed James Connolly to travel from Belfast to Wexford to see if he could negotiate a settlement. Connolly stayed in the home of Richard Corish in William Street, where he learned the mood in the town and discussed tactics. At a meeting on 2 February, Connolly declared: 'It was now time for more common sense and less abuse.' He urged the people to line the streets when the blacklegs were passing, but instead of hooting and jeering, they should look at them with scorn. He hoped that more of them might stop working for the foundries.

Connolly initiated intense behind-the-scenes negotiations using Father Hore and Cruise O'Brien, the editor of *The Free Press*. It was suggested that a new union, the Irish Foundry Workers Union, would be formed. The employers wanted a guarantee that it would have no connection with the ITGWU, but Connolly initially refused. However, on 8 February a settlement was finally agreed. The Irish Foundry Workers Union was formally established as an associate of the ITGWU. Richard Corish was blacklisted by the employers but was elected secretary of the union. Seven workers from Pierce's, seven from the Star and five from Selskar would form the union committee. There was to be no victimization and the workers were to be reinstated through the new union.

There was jubilation in the town when word of the settlement got out. Bonfires were lit and, commencing at 7.30pm, an enormous torch-lit victory procession made its way to the Town Hall (now Wexford Arts Centre). From there, the parade, led by the Irish National Foresters Brass & Reed Band and St Brigid's Fife & Drum Band, continued to the Faythe, where James Connolly addressed the elated crowd of over 5,000. *The People* carried Connolly's speech in full which he ended with: 'You will continue to march until you have acquired not only the right to be protected by unions but until you of the working class have acquired the right to own the country you are living in.'

The blacklegs departed Wexford by train and some by steamship soon after the settlement was reached. Some were attacked as they left their accommodation in Brien & Keating's, leaving through a back door into Anne Street. They needed RIC protection as they headed along the quay until James Connolly arrived and attempted to defuse the situation.

The lockout marked a victory for workers but had caused widespread poverty in the town. Within a month of returning to work the men negotiated a three-shilling per week wage increase. By 1914, the new union became affiliated with the ITGWU and this was recognized by the employers – something they swore they would never do. P. T. Daly served just one month in Waterford Jail and returned to a hero's welcome in Wexford.

The Lockout Gate Memorial in the Faythe, designed by local sculptor Peter Hodnett. It was unveiled by President Michael D. Higgins in 2012 to mark the centenary of the end of the lockout. (photo: Des Kiely)

The Dublin lockout of 20,000 workers in 1913, instigated by Jim Larkin, led to the formation of the Irish Citizen Army by Connolly and Larkin. The ICA took part in the 1916 Easter Rising, resulting in the execution of Connolly.

Richard Corish was elected Mayor of Wexford in 1920 and became the country's longest serving, remaining in the post until his death in 1945. His son, Brendan, was leader of the Labour Party from 1960-77.

By Hook or by Crooke: the sinking of the *Great Lewis*

THE CONFEDERATE Catholic Association of Ireland set up its headquarters in Kilkenny, from where it ruled two-thirds of Ireland for seven years between 1642 and 1649. This was the only decade prior to 1922 that Ireland enjoyed independence from England. In a successful attack on Duncannon Fort in 1645, the Confederates laid siege to the military stronghold for two months. Oliver Cromwell sent four ships to Duncannon with extra troops and supplies. But the Irish unleashed a sustained attack on the vessels from a strategic position above the fort, which resulted in the sinking of his flagship, the *Great Lewis*. The successful engagement by cannon fire was a huge morale boost for the Confederates.

Charles I, who succeeded to the throne in 1625 as King of England, Scotland and Ireland, believed in the divine right of kings and ruled as an absolute monarch. Shortly after his accession, he married 15-year-old Henrietta Maria, a French Catholic princess. The English parliament as well as the Puritans, who sought to emancipate the Church of England from Roman Catholic practices, opposed the marriage, fearing that Charles would undermine the reformed Church of England.

From 1632 to 1640, the king's right-hand man in Ireland was Thomas Wentworth, Earl of Strafford, who was Lord Deputy of Ireland. Wentworth administered with a heavy hand and continued the confiscation of land from Catholics for Protestant English and Scottish settlers. However, he trained up a large Catholic army in support of the king, but this was used by the Parliamentarians to accuse him of high treason for planning to use this army to subjugate England. The Parliament was afraid Ireland could become a backdoor for an invasion of England by Spanish or French forces. He was put on trial and although the case collapsed, he was nevertheless declared guilty and sentenced to death. Charles, fearing for the safety of his family, reluctantly agreed to the sentence and Wentworth was beheaded on 12 May 1641.

The establishment of the Confederation of Kilkenny was in opposition to the colonization of Ireland through the plantations that had continued from the 16th century. The Confederates, composed of Irish Catholic upper classes and clergy, tried to seize control of the English administration in Ireland and sought the establishment of Catholicism as the state religion in Ireland and to force concessions for Catholics. They professed allegiance to Charles I of England, who had promised them some concessions following the failed Catholic Rebellion which broke out in Ulster in October 1641 and raged until May the following year. The Confederate Wars, also known as the Eleven Years' War, lasted until 1653 with one-third of the country under the Confederates. In the south-east, Richard Butler (Viscount Mountgarret) brought Kilkenny, Tipperary, Waterford and Wexford under Confederate control. Butler was appointed president of the council of the Confederate Assembly.

In Wexford, over 1,500 local men mobilized in the town to support the Confederate rebels. David Synnot, who would later be made Governor of Wexford, joined the Confederates and was appointed Colonel. In 1642, Butler ordered Protestants out of Wexford and on one occasion a ship evacuating about 80 Protestant refugees out of Wexford sank with the loss of all on board. Confederate privateers operated out of Wexford, plundering English Parliamentary ships and disrupting shipping between Dublin and Liverpool. A percentage of their plunder was contributed to the Confederate government in Kilkenny. When sailors out of Wexford were captured by Parliamentary ships, they were thrown overboard with their hands tied. The Confederates in Wexford responded by threatening to kill over 150 English prisoners held in Wexford Castle if such carnage continued. Wexford therefore became a key target for the Parliamentarians and the behaviour of the Confederates in Wexford would not be forgotten by Oliver Cromwell seven years later.

Also in 1642, about 1,000 Confederate rebels were unsuccessful in an attack on Duncannon Fort. At Redmond (Loftus) Hall, they killed 150 English soldiers in a surprise ambush. In retaliation, eighteen Confederates were hanged at Ramsgrange Castle and the village burnt to the ground. The killing continued when Confederates in turn hanged eighteen English soldiers at Dungulph, near Fethard.

In 1643, the Confederates and Royalists in Ireland signed a treaty joining forces against the English Parliament. The troops stationed at the strategic Duncannon Fort, however, were found to have switched sides from being initially loyal to the Royalists to the side of the Parliamentarians. On 20 January 1645, the Confederates under General Thomas Preston, commander

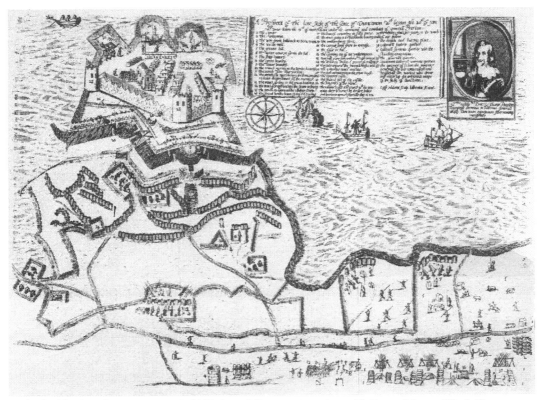

A sketch of the siege of Duncannon Fort in 1645. (From Philip Hore's 1901 'History of the Town and County of Wexford')

The Great Lewis under attack by the Confederate Catholics at Duncannon Fort. (From the collection of the Marquis of Ormonde, reproduced in Philip Hore's 1901 'History of the Town and County of Wexford')

of the Leinster Confederate Army, laid siege to Duncannon. The governor of the fort was Laurence Esmonde, now in his mid-seventies. Esmonde, a convert to Protestantism, was the second son of Walter Esmonde of Johnstown Castle and had been governor since 1606. The 1,500 Confederate soldiers surrounded the walled fort on its landward side for two months, cutting off food supplies and its fresh water source outside the walls to 200 garrison troops.

Four English supply ships, the *Great Lewis*, a 400-ton flagship of the Parliamentary navy, and its sister ships the *Mayflower*, the *Mary* and the *Elizabeth* arrived with arms, ammunition and food supplies on 24 January. The *Great Lewis* was a merchant ship hired by the navy less than a year earlier in February 1644 to guard the Irish coast. The Parliamentarians were desperate to build up a navy and hired a substantial number of merchant ships, which they fitted with extra cannon for their new role as warships and recruited extra sailors to man them.

The three sister ships managed to sail away again safely but the captain of the *Great Lewis*, Thomas Beale, unaware that the stronghold was besieged, brought his ship too close to the fort. From a clifftop, the Confederates bombarded the two-decker ship with cannon fire. In an attempt to get away, with the tide against them, the crew severed the anchor cables but the ship and its masts continued to be hit by mortar fire. The *Great Lewis* drifted out of control and out of firing range of the Confederates. After two days she sank with all hands, about a mile south-east of the fort. This was a huge morale boost for the Catholic Confederates. Having received extra troops and supplies, Duncannon Fort managed to hold out until St. Patrick's Day 1645 when it finally surrendered to the Confederates.

After defeats by the Parliamentarians and its New Model Army led by Oliver Cromwell, Charles I was imprisoned and put on trial for treason on 20 January 1649 at Westminster Hall. He was beheaded ten days later, having been found guilty and the monarchy was abolished. Four years later Cromwell became Lord Protector – King in all but name.

The protagonists in the Wars of the Three Kingdoms (England, Ireland and Scotland): Oliver Cromwell (left) for the Puritan Parliamentarians and King Charles I.

He led military campaigns to re-establish English control over Ireland (1649-50) and Scotland (1650-51). However, his massacre of defenders and civilians of Drogheda and Wexford left an indelible bloody stain on his reputation – one that Ireland would never forget.

Cromwell, with 12,000 infantry and cavalry, landed at Dublin in August 1649. After a sojourn in the city, they headed north to Drogheda the following month and laid siege to the town. Drogheda was held by the Irish Catholic Confederates and English Royalists under the command of Sir Arthur Aston. When the town refused to surrender, about 2,000 people were massacred. When Aston surrendered at Millmount Fort, he was killed by Parliamentarian soldiers, who are said to have bashed his brains out with his own wooden leg.

Next in Cromwell's sight was the Confederate town of Wexford that had been loyal to Charles I. His New Model Army first took Rosslare Fort on 2 October. They then positioned their heavy artillery on Trespan Rock just south of Wexford town and aimed their guns at Wexford Castle. After a week of negotiations with Colonel David Synnot, the Wexford garrison commander and town's governor, Cromwell's troops had grown impatient and stormed the town on 11 October, killing an estimated 2,000 soldiers and 1,500 civilians.

Meanwhile, Cromwell sent his son-in-law Henry Ireton to secure the Waterford Estuary in order to have heavy artillery moved in by the Parliamentarian navy to attack Waterford, the most important major port still held by the Royalists. Duncannon Fort and Ballyhack Castle lay on the Wexford side of the estuary and on the Waterford side stood Crooke Castle and Passage Fort. Cromwell is said to have vowed to take Waterford 'by Hook or by Crooke'. (The phrase was first recorded in 1380).

Ireton, who was married to Cromwell's eldest daughter Bridget, was appointed Major-General in the New Model Army in Ireland. The Parliamentarians under Ireton besieged Duncannon Fort, which commanded the sea passage into Waterford, for three weeks from 15 October. But the fort's garrison, under the command of Colonel Edward Wogan, himself a defector from Ireton's ranks under Cromwell, held out. The Parliamentarians' field guns were not powerful enough to breach Duncannon's walls and two of the guns were actually captured on 5 November by Duncannon's Confederate garrison. This failure by the Parliamentarians prevented them moving their heavy artillery up to Waterford by sea. Ireton's troops abandoned the siege and marched back to New Ross to rejoin Cromwell.

Cromwell had constructed a bridge of boats over the River Barrow at New Ross that enabled his troops to carry on into County Kilkenny and via Carrick-on-Suir towards Waterford. But first he sent troops to capture Passage Fort on the west bank of the Waterford Estuary. This finally allowed English ships to sail safely with their siege artillery along the western bank for the assault on Waterford. But hit by extremely bad weather, the attack on Waterford was abandoned. Cromwell's exhausted army suffered up to 1,000 deaths from an epidemic of malaria and dysentery during the winter of 1649-50.

Cromwell next took Kilkenny in March 1650 and Clonmel in May, after which he returned to England to deal with a threat from the Royalists and Covenanters in Scotland. Henry Ireton succeeded him as Lord Deputy and Commander-in-Chief of military forces in Ireland.

Henry Ireton, who took over the command of Cromwell's army to complete his conquest of Ireland.

Thomas Preston was now governor of Waterford. With plague ravaging the city that was now surrounded by English troops and fewer than 700 soldiers to man the city walls, he surrendered to Ireton on 6 August. Duncannon Fort also capitulated a week later. The siege of Limerick the following year cost the lives of 2,000 English soldiers and at least twice as many Irish soldiers and citizens, mostly from disease. Ireton himself fell ill and died on 26 November in Limerick.

The last major town in Irish hands was Galway

and the city, under Thomas Preston, surrendered in May 1652 to the Parliamentarians under Charles Cooke, and so the subjugation of Ireland was virtually complete. Catholicism was banned in Ireland and all Catholic-owned land was confiscated and given to Protestant Scottish and English settlers. So began many decades of poverty and suffering for the Irish people.

Cromwell, as Lord Protector, died at the age of 59 in 1658. Charles II, who had been living in exile, returned to England to assume the throne in 1660. He had the bodies of Oliver Cromwell and Henry Ireton exhumed from Westminster Abbey and mutilated in a posthumous execution. They had both signed the death warrant of his father Charles I twelve years earlier. Cromwell's head was put on display on top of a pole outside Westminster Hall and remained there for more than 20 years.

THE WRECK OF THE *GREAT LEWIS*

When the Port of Waterford was carrying out dredging works 350 years later in 1999, old oak timbers were exposed just eight metres below on the seabed, which is covered in about a metre of silt. The navigational channel is dredged annually to allow safe passage for large ships. In 2002, subsequent dives by marine archaeologists revealed extensive timbers, indicating the remains of a shipwreck, lying beneath the seabed. The Underwater Archaeological Unit, part of the government's National Monuments Service, also found six cannon lying in a row, mainly buried muzzle first and sticking out of the mud. In 2012 the timbers were confirmed as dating from the mid-1600s.

Dr Connie Kelleher, the site's archaeological director, in her report on the now-protected wreck site wrote: *"The historical and archaeological value of this site cannot be over-estimated. Although it would be excellent to positively identify the wreck, the fact that these are the substantial remains of a seventeenth-century ship is what is of real significance... it is the first shipwreck from that time to be discovered and then investigated in Irish waters. The possibility that it could have been directly involved in a period of our history that has left such an immense mark adds even more importance to the wreck, as does the realisation that we could, in fact, be looking at a war grave."*

Historians are already comparing its importance to the 1971 discovery of the *Mary Rose*, Henry VIII's flagship, which sank near Portsmouth in 1545, exactly 100 years before the *Great Lewis*.

The Irish Dames who fled Ypres to Macmine Castle

The destruction of the Belgian town of Ypres during the First World War.

KNOWN as the Irish Dames of Ypres, *De Iersche Damen* in Dutch or *Les Dames Irlandaises* in French, they were the only community of Irish Benedictine nuns on the Continent. The sisters were forced to flee Belgium in 1914 following the outbreak of the First World War. After over a year in England, they settled at Macmine Castle, County Wexford, in 1916. Finally, in 1920 the community established a permanent home at Kylemore Abbey in Connemara.

The Belgian city of Ypres in West Flanders stood in the path of Germany's planned push into France from the north in 1914. The German Army surrounded the municipality on three sides while Allied forces made costly advances into German lines. The city was completely destroyed during the war, with more than 600,000 dead. Ypres was subsequently rebuilt in its original style, paid for by Germany. Along with Hiroshima, today it enjoys the title 'City of Peace'.

Catholicism was effectively outlawed in Ireland under the Penal Laws of the mid-1500s. Protestantism was declared the state religion in England and Ireland, with King Henry VIII as supreme head of the Church. It was now considered treasonous to follow the Church in Rome. Many Catholics, including wealthy nobles, fled to the Continent. Among them were the wife

and daughter of Thomas Percy, the Earl of North-
umberland, who was beheaded for treason in 1572.
He had taken part in a rebellion of Catholic nobles
to have Mary, Queen of Scots placed on the English
throne. In 1895 he was beatified by Pope Leo XIII.

Thomas Percy's wife, Anne, Countess of North-
umberland, along with her infant daughter Mary,
were forced into exile in Flanders in the Spanish
Netherlands. Mary was educated in Flanders and,
having joined the Benedictines aged 16, founded a
Benedictine community of her own in Brussels in
1598. Mary, as abbess, was known as Lady Mary
Percy. Benedictine nuns were given the title 'Dame'
and abbesses were referred to as 'Lady', while
Benedictine monks were called 'Dom'. One of the
best known is Dom Pérignon, who at this time was

*The Abbey of the Irish Dames on
Rue St. Jacques in Ypres, Belgium,
photographed in the early 1900s.*

a member of the Benedictines in France. He was in charge of his abbey's wine
cellar and is credited with having contributed to perfecting the champagne
production method.

The Benedictines in Brussels expanded rapidly and in 1665 a convent was
established in a temporary building in Ypres. Six years later they secured a
permanent monastery and school on Rue Saint-Jacques. This would be home
to the nuns in Ypres for the next 250 years. In 1682, Dame Flavia Carey was
appointed Lady Abbess and from then on the community became known as
De Iersche Damen (the Irish Dames). In 1678, Ypres was conquered by French
forces and remained under French control until 1697, when it was returned to
the Spanish Crown.

When Carey died suddenly in 1686, she was replaced as abbess by Mary
Butler, a member of the Butler dynasty of Kilkenny. Just two years later, the
Catholic monarch, King James II invited Mary and her community to return to
Ireland and establish a Benedictine abbey in Dublin. Abbess Butler and a
number of the Ypres community settled into a new enclosure on Big Sheep
Street (now known as Great Ship Street), where they established a school for
the daughters of Catholic Irish gentry. But their tenure was short lived. After
the Protestant William of Orange defeated King James at the Battle of the

Boyne in 1690, the Irish Dames returned within days to exile in Flanders.

Over the decades the convent in Ypres gained a reputation for offering a high standard of education. Many wealthy Irish Catholics were sending their daughters to board with the nuns in Ypres. However, by the early 1800s, with the easing of the Penal Laws, congregations such as the Loreto Order were opening boarding schools in Ireland. But the convent of the Irish Dames in Ypres flourished again in the second half of the century.

The troubled country of Belgium came into being following the 1830 revolution that led to its separation from the Netherlands. It was now a sovereign, Catholic, neutral state. Under the Treaty of London in 1839, the independence and neutrality of Belgium was guaranteed. French was the single official language until 1898, when Dutch also became recognized in law and is today the first language of the majority.

FIRST WORLD WAR

When Germany declared war on Russia on 1 August 1914, France ordered full mobilization the next day in support of Russia. Germany's response was to first defeat France, before shifting its forces towards Russia. To this end, Germany demanded free passage through neutral Belgium in order to achieve a swift victory over the French but this was refused. Britain was now obliged to declare war on Germany in compliance with its obligations to protect Belgium under the Treaty of London. On 4 August, German troops crossed the Belgian frontier. All German nationals were expelled from the country, including four members of the Benedictine community in Ypres, who fled to Holland. The German forces advanced rapidly, occupying over 95% of the country by October – apart from a small area around Ypres. Situated about 20 miles from the North Sea coast, Ypres stood in the path of the German Western Front's so-called 'Race to the Sea' to secure the

All that remained of the convent and school in Ypres when the First World War ended in 1918.

ports. In the intense First Battle of Ypres (October-November 1914), between the German Army and Belgian, French and British forces, the city was destroyed. Casualties on both sides from fighting in the area totalled about 300,000 dead.

The Irish Dames provided shelter to wounded French soldiers and people fleeing the violence, accommodating over 50 people nightly. But as the fighting intensified, the ailing abbess, Belgian-born Lady Abbess Bergé, aged 84, and two elderly sisters were removed to La Sainte Union convent in nearby Poperinge. This was in late October 1914 and the abbess had not been outside the enclosure for sixty years. The remaining fourteen nuns followed a week later, walking the nine miles to Poperinge, where they too were given shelter for the following two weeks. On 22 November, fighting was suspended and the Benedictine nuns managed to reach Boulogne and from there sailed to Folkestone.

After a brief stay in London they accepted a long-standing invitation from the Benedictine Abbey in Oulton in Staffordshire, where they remained for six months. From there they returned to London and for the next nine months stayed with the Daughters of Wisdom at Highfield House in Golders Green. Meanwhile in Ypres, the abbey of the Irish Dames was completely gutted by fire. Ypres was now known as the 'city of the dead' after enduring relentless shelling and gas attacks. But the nuns had fully intended to return to Ypres after the war ended. Dame Columban wrote in 1915: *And now, what has God in store for us? We know not! When shall we return to brave little Belgium, and how shall*

Irish Dames of Ypres. The prioress, Dame Maura Ostyn (front row, centre) and Dame Teresa (back row, second from right) travelled together to Ireland in search of accommodation for their community, who were in exile in England from Belgium.

we rebuild our monastery which, as has been said, should this very year celebrate its 250th anniversary?'

During their stay in Highfield, the sisters had a visit from Dom Columba Marmion, the Benedictine abbot of Maredsous Abbey near Namur in Belgium, who had fled with his novices in 1915. They were now settled in Edermine House near Enniscorthy, where they would remain until the conclusion of the war. Dom Marmion suggested to the prioress, Dame Maura, that they should consider establishing a convent in Ireland.

A substantial property, Merton House, was for sale in Macmine, about two miles from Edermine, and he thought this was worth viewing. The prioress agreed and decided to travel to County Wexford, accompanied by Dame Teresa (Dora Howard), who was a niece of the Irish Parliamentary Party leader John Redmond. Redmond had written to the Bishop of Ferns, John Browne, expressing his 'personal interest in this community, by reason of the fact that my niece is a member of it'. Through donations, Dame Teresa published a book in 1915 entitled *'The Irish Nuns at Ypres: an episode of the war'*, with a foreword by her uncle, John Redmond.

ARRIVAL IN MACMINE

Merton, the former home of Arthur Eden, a Justice of the Peace, overlooked the River Slaney and stood close to Macmine Castle. The castle, originally a Norman tower house, was built by the prominent FitzHenry family but confiscated in 1654 following the Cromwellian conquest. It was acquired by Pierce King, from whom nearby King's Island on the Slaney derives its name. The King family sold the property to John Richards in 1860, who extended and adapted it into a medieval style castle. Merton House stood on 40 acres but the house had not been lived in for two years and the gardens were overgrown. However, Dame Maura Ostyn was impressed and signed a lease on the property in February 1916.

While the First World War continued in Europe, the Easter Rising erupted in Dublin on 24 April. The Benedictine nuns were busy trying to set up their new home in Macmine when Edermine Bridge was blown up on 27 April, coinciding with the outbreak of rebellion in Enniscorthy. Provisions now had to be transported from Wexford by boat. The Rising also impacted financially on the sisters. Redmond's influence was brought to an end, affecting their

Macmine Castle was home to the Irish Dames of Ypres from 1916 to 1920.

appeals through him for funding the establishment of their new convent and school. The War Refugees Committee granted the nuns ten shillings each per week for the duration of the war in Europe.

The *Wexford People* reported in August 1916 that the first postulants at Merton received the white veil. They were Kate Magner from Cork and local girl Maggie Curtis from Knockduff, Bree. The nuns farmed the land themselves and in September two girls were entrusted to them for their education. They were at first taught informally, becoming the first pupils. Lady Abbess Bergé died in November 1916 aged 86 and the prioress, Dame Ostyn, was elected the new abbess.

The community decided that Merton House should become the school and the nuns would rent Macmine Castle and that would become their home. They renovated and painted the house and planned to open the school to boarding as well as day pupils in September 1917. When they opened, the roll book was full, 30 girls having enrolled. A number of the boarders were themselves refugees from Belgium.

Dame Teresa's uncle, Major William Redmond, was killed in action at Ypres in June 1917 and is remembered in Redmond Park in Wexford. He was MP for East Clare for 25 years. In March 1918, the death of Willie's brother, John Redmond in London was announced. His funeral was held in Westminster Cathedral and his remains returned to Ireland on the RMS *Leinster*, arriving in Kingstown. A train draped in black cloth travelled in procession to Wexford, carrying his body for interment in the family vault in St John's Graveyard. The

Benedictine nuns knelt on the platform in prayer as the train passed slowly through Macmine Junction.

In November 1918, the Spanish flu, brought to Ireland by troops returning from Europe, claimed the lives of Sister Mary (Kate Magner), who was professed at Merton in 1916, and Mary Burke, a lay teacher who had joined the teaching staff when the school opened the previous year. The war in Europe finally ended in that same month but returning to Ypres was out of the question for the nuns as their old convent had been completely destroyed.

The community gained eleven new entrants in their time in Macmine and the school was full to capacity. However, conditions in Merton House and Macmine Castle were less than adequate. The school was cold and damp and the cost of heating and running both properties was a continuous drain on their funds. The castle, which they were renting, was in need of major renovations. A decision was made to seek larger, more suitable accommodation. In 1919, the Archbishop of Tuam suggested that Kylemore Castle in Connemara, which was up for sale, might suit. As the War of Independence raged throughout the country, the Abbess and Dame Teresa travelled to County Galway and were very impressed with what they found.

Kylemore was built for the Henry family in 1868 and set on over 10,000 acres in a breathtaking location near the village of Letterfrack. In 1903 it was sold to the Duke of Manchester, and again put up for sale in 1914.

From an asking price of £150,000, the nuns finally clinched the deal for £45,000. In December 1920, local people in Macmine saw the 23 nuns off as they headed with their belongings for the train to Clifden. The castle became Kylemore Abbey, an exclusive boarding and day school for girls and operated until 2010, when it was forced to close.

Today, Macmine Castle lies in ruin, the demesne having been purchased in 1944 for farmland by the Flood family. It was acquired by the Dunnes in 1965, who continue to farm there today.

The Irish Nuns of Ypres

The Irish Benedictine Dames of the Royal Abbey of the Immaculate Conception, at Ypres, have, with the cordial approval of His Lordship the BISHOP OF FERNS, opened a Select Boarding-School, similar to that which they directed for so many years in Belgium.

It is their aim to instil into their Pupils a fervent and solid piety, without which true education cannot exist; together with a judicious notion of personal responsibility—at the same time developing the intellectual and moral qualities.

The Course of Studies comprises all the branches of a superior education, **with the advantages of a continental training.** The system of teaching is adapted to ensure for each Pupil thoroughness in every branch.

Careful attention is given to health, diet and recreation. The neighbourhood is well-known for its beautiful scenery, and the children enjoy a great variety of walks.

For further details and Prospectus apply to—

REV LADY ABBESS, O.S.B.,

Ypres Benedictine Abbey,

Macmine Castle, Co. Wexford.

An advertisement for their school in Macmine, placed by the nuns in the Irish Times in 1917.

Twelve brave men resisted eviction in Coolroe, Ballycullane

An RIC constable aims his rifle with fixed bayonet at one of the men who is refusing to leave the fortified two-storey house of Tom Somers, nicknamed Somers Fort. These photographs are from a re-enactment by constables from Tintern barracks, taken a couple of days after the eviction. (photos: Robert French/NLI)

THOMAS SOMERS was 34 years old in 1888. He had married widow Ellen Rossiter six years earlier and between them they had six children at the time. Their home, a two-storey slated farmhouse, was in the townland of Coolroe near Ballycullane on the Tintern Estate.

In post-Famine Ireland, evictions increased after the passing of the Poor Law Amendment Act of 1847. Landlords were now liable for a new tax on all rented property, including the smallest holdings, in order to fund the relief of the destitute. The law also included a clause that a tenant could not continue to reside in a property where the rent had not been paid. Landlords increased the rents and where the tenant was unable or unwilling to pay, widespread evictions resulted.

The Land League was formed by Michael Davitt and Charles Stewart Parnell in 1879 to fight extortionate rent increases by landlords and resist evictions. Its ultimate aim was, through agitation, the abolition of landlordism in Ireland so that tenant farmers could own the land that they worked. With William Redmond, a brother of the politician John Redmond, Davitt travelled to the

USA to fundraise for the League.

The Government's response was the Land Law Act of 1881. The new Irish Land Commission was established and tenant farmers were granted the three Fs: Fair rent, Freedom of sale and Fixity of tenure. Land courts were empowered to fix rents for 15 years and the State would advance three quarters of the purchase price of land purchase, to be repaid over 35 years. However, few tenants could afford to purchase the land. The Land League continued its agitation with their 'Plan of Campaign' of 1886-92. It called on tenants to withhold payments of rent until landlords agreed to rent reductions. If the landlord refused, the tenant would pay the rent into a fund at a rate they deemed to be fair.

In 1887, in the famous Coolgreany eviction incident in the north of the county, the tenants withheld their rent until a reduction was agreed. But their Plan of Campaign ended in tragedy when a campaigner was shot dead by one of the 'emergency-men' – the only Wexford person to die as a result of the Land War.

The parish priest of Ramsgrange, Canon Thomas Doyle, became heavily involved in the Plan of Campaign on the Hook Peninsula. Doyle was from a politically active family and was a second cousin of the 1798 leader John Kelly from Killanne. In 1887 in the townland of Ballykerogue, north of Campile and on the Tottenham Estate, David Foley was threatened with eviction when his request for a rent reduction of one quarter was refused. With the help of 21 men from the parish, the house that became known as 'Foley's Fort' was defended in vain against 'emergency-men' and police. All were later tried in Arthurstown and jailed for terms of three to six months. Among the 21 were James and Patrick Kennedy from Dunganstown, nephews of John F. Kennedy's great grandfather.

The Cistercian monks of Tintern Abbey lost possession of their lands in 1536, when the abbey was suppressed. The estate passed to the loyal Colclough family. After 300 years, they were compelled to sell off some of the estate lands to cover crippling legal costs. This followed a prolonged legal battle over the disputed will of the last patriarch of the family, Caesar Colclough, who died in 1842. James Byrne, not an Anglo-Irish Protestant landlord but an Irish Catholic, subsequently purchased large areas of the estate, including Coolroe in 1864. James Byrne, an elderly bachelor who resided in nearby Burkestown but mainly with his younger brother Michael at Rosemount, Mount Elliott near New Ross, evicted many small landholders in Coolroe. Tom Somers, one of the largest tenants, farmed 47 acres in Coolroe. He was being charged £71 annually although the valuation set under the Poor Law Valuation was £39. Because of repeated bad harvests, Somers was unable to pay, had fallen into a full year's arrears and had appealed an earlier court order to vacate the property.

THE BATTLE OF 'SOMERS FORT'

Tom Somers decided to remain on his farm and resist eviction. Friends and neighbours helped him to defend the dwelling against the expected arrival of the bailiffs. They constructed ten-foot-high banks of earth and rubble around the farmhouse to thwart the use of the battering ram. The upper windows were removed and barricaded using iron gates. The group armed themselves with iron bars, several gallons of boiling tar and water and enough food to last several days. They broke holes in the walls of the house to enable them to pour water on the attackers. Witnesses said they "wore hats somewhat of the fashion of the Texan cowboy" while defending what became known as

'Somers Fort'. Along with his brother Jim and stepson Jeremiah Rossiter, Tom was joined by:

Two RIC constables show how one of the defenders was forcibly removed through the roof.

    Michael Caul, Ballygarvan
    Patrick Finn, Ballycullane
    Patrick Fitzgerald, Coolroe,
    John Hall, Taylorstown
    Michael Morris, Ballinruane
    Thomas Power, Rathimney
    Bartle Rochford, Ballygarvan
    William Shiel, Rathimney
    Martin Tubbrit, Taylorstown.

On the night of 15 August 1888, about 150 policemen were conveyed by steamer from Waterford to Duncannon Fort. They were joined the next day by local RIC constables, escorting sheriffs and bailiffs under the command of the Resident Magistrate for Kilkenny, Heffernan Considine. The group was led by Wexford County Inspector Jones and District Inspectors O'Reilly of Taghmon and Holmes of Gorey.

Resident Magistrates were appointed following the passing of the Constabulary Act (Ireland) of 1836. The RMs were nominated and supervised by Dublin Castle to oversee the fair administration of local justice. There had been an enduring problem of corrupt and partisan local justices operating throughout the country. During the Land Wars of the 1880s, the RMs became peacekeepers as well as judges and their job became more demanding and sometimes dangerous.

It was after nine o'clock in the morning when the St Martin's Fife and Drum Band (Tintern), flying the Green flag and the Stars and Stripes, arrived close to the farmhouse. The laneway leading to Somers' house was blocked with trees, felled the night before, to block the passage of the battering ram. The ram and scaling ladders had to be manoeuvred with difficulty through a yard belonging to the landlord. The military crowd marched the short distance from Ballycullane, followed by a large number of Land League representatives from across the county.

When the police ordered the band to stop playing, they met with refusal. They then attempted to seize the band's two flags. A baton charge ensued, involving about thirty constables under the orders of Inspector Holmes. The crowd fought back wielding sticks. A fair offer on behalf of Tom Somers was made to the elderly landlord, James Byrne, known locally as 'The Hermit', but it was vigorously turned down. The RM appealed to those inside the house not to resist the sheriff or bailiffs. But the men refused to come out and responded with cries of "Hurrah for the Plan!" and "Let the ram come on!"

It was 10.30am when the enforcers dragged forward the scaling ladders and battering ram – a large tree trunk – and propelled it with force to break through the wall of the dwelling. Four times they were beaten back down the sloping earthen banks. The police were armed with batons and fixed bayonets on their rifles against the unarmed men who had barricaded themselves inside. According to *The Freeman's Journal* reporting on the incident, *'The Emergency blackguards, under the leadership of the head blackguard, Woods, were made light work of by the garrison.'* *The People* newspaper wrote: *'Rotten eggs, cold and hot water, were showered on the heads of the emergency-men who grew purple with rage, as they met with defeat and disaster at every step.'* Stones were thrown from the roof and the emergency-men replied with same.

The stone-throwing continued for some time and the crowd cheered every time the emergency-men were forced back down the earthen embankment. Among the witnesses to the fighting were Canon Doyle, Father Roice from St Leonard's, Father Kavanagh from Gusserane, Father Walsh from Terrerath and Father Furlong from Passage East. Suddenly, Willie Redmond MP rushed into the yard, hat in hand, shouting to the defenders: "Well

Willie Redmond (left) and his brother John in 1912. They were both present at and encouraged the Coolroe siege. (photo: NLI)

done my lads, well done. Wexford forever!" The RM complained that he would not tolerate his language. Willie Redmond had spent three months in Kilmainham Jail, along with Land League president Charles Stewart Parnell and political activist John Dillon in 1882.

With tensions rising, Willie's brother, the politician John Redmond, appeared from the crowd, along with John Dillon and Edward Walsh, editor of *The People* newspaper. A final attempt was made with the battering ram to penetrate the wall of the house but this again ended in failure. The emergency-men fell back, wiping their eyes from the sheep dip that was showered on them. The officials then ordered the police to take the house by force and a bayonet charge was ordered.

The police climbed onto the roof but were three times beaten back by the defenders inside using iron bars and sticks. One policeman was injured when he fell back off the top of the roof and others tumbled down the earthen banks, sustaining cuts and bruises. The men looked down from the roof and dared the police up for another fight. Canon Doyle and the Redmonds continued to shout "cowards!" at the police and protested to RM Considine, who had ordered the use of bayonets. Meanwhile, the landlord stood leaning on his stick and next to a police constable in fear of what was ensuing around him.

Canon Doyle appealed to Byrne to reconsider the offer made earlier to resolve the dispute. His tenants had offered to pay their rents and arrears at Government valuations. But Byrne would have none of it, saying "I don't want to be robbed at all."

It was almost nightfall when a final attempt by about fifty policemen to take the fortified dwelling by force was decided upon. A desperate struggle took place, with the defenders throwing crowbars through the breaches that they had made in the walls of the house. The constables were sprayed with hot water and tar and forced back down the embankment, covered in blood and dirt, and some temporarily blinded. The fighting lasted for half an hour as the large crowd looked on, cheering wildly.

The RM now threatened to use live bullets if the men inside continued to refuse to surrender. Canon Doyle then climbed to one of the breaches in the house and asked the men inside to comply. They finally agreed, on condition that they would be allowed to walk out with all the honours of war. The men climbed down the earthen bank, to be warmly greeted by well-wishers before being handcuffed. They were taken to Arthurstown barracks that evening and remanded there. Three days later they were moved to Wexford Jail.

THE TRIAL IN ARTHURSTOWN

The following month, the men were conveyed to Arthurstown Courthouse to stand trial. On the opening day of the trial, up to 6,000 supporters had gathered in the village and along the approach roads. The crowd cheered on a number of bands present, including the New Ross Brass Band. Although Canon Doyle had ordered public houses to remain shut for the duration of the trial, alcohol was passed among the exuberant crowd. The police and

The aftermath of the eviction and the battering ram (a tree trunk) used in an attempt to smash through the walls of Tom Somers' house.

military presence numbered about 300 and houses and roads into the village were festooned with green buntings and banners proclaiming 'Hurrah for the defenders of Somers Fort'.

When the twelve handcuffed prisoners arrived from Wexford under police guard, the people were ecstatic. Some scuffles broke out between civilians and police. When Willie and John Redmond, John Dillon and other Land League members followed, they were greeted with loud cheers. The small courtroom was crammed full. The prisoners were positioned side by side across the courtroom. Thirty policemen were in charge of the men and about thirty members of the public were admitted, along with members of the press.

The trial before the Resident Magistrate, Heffernan Considine, lasted six days and resulted in sentences of between three and six months with hard labour being handed down to each of the men. Jim Somers was sentenced to a further four months for assaulting a policeman. The prisoners were returned to Wexford by train and were met at the station by cheering crowds, who followed them and their police escort as they were marched to the jail on Spawell Road.

On the day after the trial ended in Arthurstown, Willie Redmond MP was brought before Wexford Court, charged with inciting the Coolroe defenders to resist the sheriff and bailiffs. He was sentenced to three months in jail with hard labour. Redmond addressed the magistrates, saying "I undoubtedly cheered the men defending their homes against unjust eviction, and I will cheer every man who defends his home against unjust eviction", which was followed by applause from his supporters. The judge flew into a rage and ordered the court to be cleared. When Redmond was removed from the courthouse a crowd of people lining the quay cheered as he was escorted to the jail to join the Coolroe prisoners.

Only Bartle Rochford, Patrick Finn and Martin Tubbrit served their sentences in Wexford Jail. When Rochford and Finn were released in March 1889, they were greeted at the Redmond Monument by a large crowd that was addressed by the freed pair. Tom Somers and Michael Morris were released from Kilkenny Jail the following month. They were met by St Martin's Fife and Drum Band and a crowd of well-wishers. William Shiel, John Hall and Michael Caul were released from Kilmainham Jail in Dublin and Thomas Power from Dundalk Jail on the same day. They all arrived home to rapturous cheers from waiting throngs of hundreds of supporters.

Jim Somers, the last Coolroe prisoner to be set free, completed three months of his sentence in Wexford Jail and the rest in Kilmainham. On his release he was met by his brother Tom and friend Michael Morris. They boarded the train from Harcourt Street to New Ross, where the St Martin's Band again entertained the assembled crowd that had gathered to greet them, just as they had done a year previously during the Coolroe siege.

THE AFTERMATH

Although the struggle at Somers Fort ended in eviction, the battering ram was defeated for the first time that day. The families who lost their homes were forced to live for the next twenty years in temporary wooden huts erected by fellow supporters of the Land League. James Byrne was henceforth shunned by the community and ten years after the Coolroe siege he died still refusing to relent, even on his deathbed. It was another ten years before *The Free Press* could report in 1908 that 'There is peace in Coolroe at last; the tenants are once more in possession of their homes and lands'.

The Wyndham Land Act of 1903, also known as the Irish Land Purchase Act, and the appointment of an Estates Commission were genuine attempts to finally solve the Irish land question. George Wyndham was the Chief Secretary for Ireland from 1900-05 and under his new law tenants could purchase land titles. The scheme allowed for the Government to pay the difference between the price offered by the tenant and that demanded by the landlord. The law ushered in the most radical change in the history of land ownership in Ireland. The United Irish League, whose motto was 'The Land for the People', was founded in 1898. The League represented the tenants before the Estates Commission.

George Wyndham was credited for ushering in the radical 1903 Land Act that enabled tenants to purchase land with the help of government subsidies.

On 20 March 1908, the evicted Coolroe tenants were formally handed possession of their old lands by the Estates Commission inspector, R.H. Barrington. All received an increase in acreage to what they had formerly rented. Each tenant was handed a piece of sod and a twig from his land, symbolizing ownership and hopefully the end of their suffering. Tears ran down the wrinkled cheeks of some of the old veterans of the Land War as they were handed possession on a day they thought they might never live to see. Free government grants enabled them to repair their old homes, rebuild those that had been demolished and restock their farms. If the grant was insufficient, they could borrow money on their own personal security at very low terms.

Canon Thomas Doyle did not live to see his parishioners regain possession of their properties. He died aged 86 in 1903 but is remembered for his resolute support for the Land League and its Plan of Campaign. Limerick-born Heffernan Considine became Resident Magistrate for counties Kerry and Kilkenny and was appointed Deputy Inspector-General of the RIC in 1900. Willie Redmond was killed in action in Flanders in 1917 during World War One. Redmond Memorial Park, a short distance from the jail where he served his sentence, was dedicated to him in 1931. A statue of Redmond, erected inside the entrance gate, was sculpted by Oliver Sheppard who was also responsible for the Pikeman statue in the Bullring.

The Coolroe eviction was immortalized in several verses and songs. The travelling Wexford bard, Michael O'Brien, composed the poem 'The Evictions of Coolroe' with the opening lines: *"On the sixth of September long we remember, the days upon all our prisoners did go. Relieved from their sentences nobly defending the house of Tom Somers who lives in Coolroe".*

The British administration departed a century ago but the Somers are still resident in Coolroe. Helen Stafford, the great-granddaughter of Tom Somers, is the fourth generation to live in the 300-year-old farmhouse and now operates Somers Fort Holidays in converted outbuildings on the property.

The 300-year-old house 'Somers Fort' is today home to Helen Stafford, great-granddaughter of Tom Somers. (photo: Des Kiely)

When a divided Enniscorthy erupted into Civil War in 1922

A Free State Army garrison held out here in Enniscorthy Castle for three days and nights under a barrage of gunfire from anti-Treaty IRA forces. Historic Vinegar Hill can be seen in the distance. (photo: W.A. Green/National Museums NI)

THE ANGLO-IRISH TREATY, signed in December 1921, followed the declaration of a truce in the War of Independence six months earlier. The Treaty was narrowly ratified by a fractured Dáil in January 1922, with opponents of the agreement abstaining. It became effective on 31 March 1922, but the political division led to Civil War in June.

While thousands of British Army soldiers remained in Dublin awaiting evacuation from the country, the Four Courts was occupied two weeks later by approximately 200 anti-Treaty forces. Led by Rory O'Connor, they held the building for nearly eleven weeks, hoping to reignite the fight against the British. Quartermaster of the garrison was Liam Mellows, whose mother Sarah was a native of Monalug, Inch, County Wexford.

On 28 June, the Free State Army under Michael Collins, and with artillery borrowed from the British, attacked the Four Courts. When commander Paddy O'Brien was injured, Ernie O'Malley took command. After two days of fighting the building was on fire and O'Malley was forced to surrender to the Free State troops. The anti-Treaty faction lost three men during the bombardment and centuries of irreplaceable documents held in the Public Record Office were destroyed in the ensuing fire.

Ernie O'Malley escaped capture. But four of the leading Republicans – Rory O'Connor, Liam Mellows, Richard Barrett and Joe McKelvey – after being in custody for five months, were executed by the Free State in December 1922.

Civil War was effectively declared when the Four Courts was attacked by the Free State Army. The conflict spread throughout the country, with Republicans holding for the first number of weeks Waterford, Cork and Limerick, which they called the 'Munster Republic'. Having been relatively dormant during the War of Independence, County Wexford now experienced a particularly violent period, which lasted until May 1923. Flying columns were formed to disrupt the movement of Free State troops in the county. Railway lines were destroyed and roads and bridges damaged. Many RIC barracks and seven 'big houses' were gutted in arson attacks.

Ernie O'Malley, now on the run, continued the guerrilla warfare in the capital with the Dublin Brigade. He had fought in 1916 but was now disillusioned by what he saw as a lack of tactics in the occupation of the Four Courts. He believed that the men should have held the approaches to the building and taken the fighting onto the streets. He also felt a failure, having surrendered his own command. *'I was annoyed by this calm acceptance of our lack of planning as heroism,'* he later wrote.

O'Malley's men escaped the Free State Army's cordon around Dublin and regrouped in Blessington, County Wicklow. A column of men under his command was summoned to Enniscorthy, stopping first in Carlow.

Free State troops were based in Enniscorthy Castle, the RIC Barracks and Enniscorthy Post Office. When news of the fighting in the Four Courts reached Wexford, instructions were issued to the local brigade

The old Enniscorthy RIC Barracks. Now demolished, it served as the Garda Station after the Civil War. (detail from Lawrence Collection/NLI)

The belfry of St Mary's Church was occupied by anti-Treaty IRA snipers. (detail from Lawrence Collection/NLI)

to attack the military positions. The anti-Treaty IRA, who already occupied the Courthouse, now took over the Council Offices on Market Square and St Mary's Church of Ireland, which overlooked the castle. Snipers took up positions in the church belfry. The water supply to the Castle was cut off, in the hope that the troops would be forced to eventually surrender. The Free Staters in turn occupied Lett's Brewery on Mill Park Road; this gave them a commanding view over the Courthouse.

At around 10pm on Sunday night, 2 July, a gunfight between the St Mary's Church snipers and Free State soldiers in the Castle and RIC Barracks erupted. Lett's Brewery was also targeted, forcing the Free Staters to retreat. By the next morning, most of the surrounding streets had been evacuated by terrified residents, while some remained locked in their homes. The shooting became so intense that people trying to make their way to the train station were forced to take a circuitous route and cross the Slaney by boat – too scared to cross the old bridge. According to the *New Ross Standard*, '*Some people to make assurance doubly sure walked to Edermine and took the train to Enniscorthy to accomplish the short distance between their homes in Mill Park Road and the railway station.*'

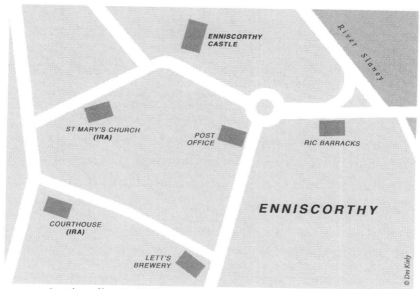

Locations of key sites held in Enniscorthy during the fighting on 2-5 July 1922.

Gunfire persisted with shooting coming from various positions around the town. The Free State soldiers returned fire with heavy guns, and grenades thrown from the roof of the Castle. The IRA exploded a mine in front of the Castle but it caused only minor damage. Help was requested from IRA forces outside the town. The attacks continued into Tuesday and by now the anti-Treaty IRA numbered several hundred. They had encircled the Free State troops

Enniscorthy Post Office with the castle in the background. Both were garrisoned by Free State troops. (photo: Des Kiely)

in the Castle and the RIC Barracks and were sporadically firing on them.

At around 3am on Wednesday, the third day of the siege, a large IRA unit from Tipperary, commanded by Michael Sheehan, reached the town. In the darkness, they took up rifle and machine-gun positions on Abbey Quay, having taken possession of some corn stores directly opposite the RIC Barracks.

Less than two hours later, Ernie O'Malley's men arrived. They included other escapees of the Four Courts siege, among them Seán Lemass and his former commander Paddy O'Brien. They moved from house to house in the vicinity of the Castle and occupied positions to the rear of the Barracks.

O'Malley, Paddy O'Brien and others rushed up Friary Lane behind the Post Office. Believing the premises to be occupied by Free State soldiers, they smashed windows with their rifle butts and hurled in hand grenades. A sniper in Kehoe's public house on Castle Hill responded, hitting two of the IRA men. Maurice Spillane, a local volunteer from Hospital Lane, lay flat on his back, dying. He attempted to recite an Act of Contrition as he passed away. In the War of Independence, Maurice had been a member of the North Wexford flying column. Paddy O'Brien was also hit and carried away to the dressing station on Court Street, with blood flowing from his neck. He was lying on the floor, bleeding through his bandages. *'Don't talk to him,'* a Cumann na mBan volunteer whispered; *'he's been shot through the lung.'*

Ernie O'Malley's comrades collected petrol and explosives, intent on blowing off the front gate the Castle, and then the front door. A deputation of priests came to speak to O'Malley, requesting him to call a ceasefire and withdraw from the town. He responded by telling them he was there as a soldier and if they wanted to prevent any more bloodshed, they ought to tell the Free State garrison to surrender. *'Otherwise they haven't much hope,'* he said. The priests agreed to talk with the Free Staters and so O'Malley called a one-hour ceasefire.

At about 4pm a Free State officer carrying a white flag was led blindfolded to IRA headquarters. *'I wish to arrange terms of surrender,'* he said. The fighting had now come to a dramatic end. In the partially-collapsed and bullet-ridden RIC Barracks, Brigadier N. J. Murphy called on his 26-man garrison to cease fire. They were followed by the 10-man garrison in the Castle under Staff Captain, Seán Gallagher.

The IRA drew a cordon around the Castle and Barracks to allow an ambulance through. A number of injured soldiers were taken to the County Home (later known as St John's Hospital). There were no deaths among the Free State force.

The soldiers drew up two deep outside the Castle and surrendered their arms. O'Malley allowed them keep their revolvers. *'The officers, one by one, gave me their solemn promise that they would not bear arms against the Republican forces again; their men gave a promise to their officers,'* recalled O'Malley in his memoirs. The IRA agreed that there would be no rejoicing or celebrating. They shook hands with the defeated soldiers and congratulated them on their coura-geous stand. They had not slept since Sunday and had remained at their posts while running low on food and water. *'We watched the greencoats march out of Enniscorthy,'* recalled O'Malley.

The amount of ord-nance and ammunition left behind by the Free State army was substan-

One of the IRA flying columns operating during the Civil War.

tial. It included a machine gun and a number of grenades. The Courthouse suffered extensive fire damage and the town was battle-scarred with many houses damaged. The walls of buildings were left with hundreds of bullet holes. The IRA smashed the roof of the Barracks to prevent it being reoccupied and armoured plates protecting the windows were carried off on lorries.

The townspeople congregated in Market Square, relieved to be again free to walk through the streets without running a gauntlet of gunfire. Nothing in the nature of rejoicing took place. The IRA men paraded in the square later that evening. They were given overnight accommodation in the town's hotels and entertained in local hostelries. When they departed the following morning, a divided Enniscorthy returned to relative normality.

The wounded IRA men were being comforted by the nuns in the County Home. Ernie O'Malley and Seán Lemass visited Paddy O'Brien, who was dying. *'Paddy,'* said O'Malley, *'we have to go. There are other posts to be cleared in this area.'* In gasps of pain, Paddy tried to speak: *'I'm sorry to leave you so soon. Fight well for Ireland. Beannacht Dé.'* As they walked away, O'Malley said to Lemass: *'The capture of this place was never worth the loss.'* Lemass replied: *'No, I wish we had never come near the damn place.'*

Ernie O'Malley returned to County Carlow, where he received a dispatch saying he had been appointed Assistant Chief of Staff, tasked with organizing Ulster and Leinster IRA units. In a shoot-out in Ballsbridge in Dublin on 4 November, he was severely wounded, having been hit over twenty times. Due to his injuries he was neither tried nor executed. But after the war ended with a nationwide ceasefire in April 1923, O'Malley was imprisoned in Mountjoy Jail. Although the fighting had ended, IRA prisoners remained in jail. He went on hunger strike for forty-one days in protest. While still incarcerated, he was elected as Sinn Féin TD for Dublin North in the 1923 general election. Seán Lemass served as Taoiseach in 1959-66.

Some quotes are taken from Ernie O'Malley's memoir, 'The Singing Flame', republished by Cormac O'Malley in 2012.

Ernie O'Malley (far left), photographed in 1934 by his future wife Helen Hooker. Above: their son Cormac with the author in 2019.

ASSAULT AT FERRYCARRIG

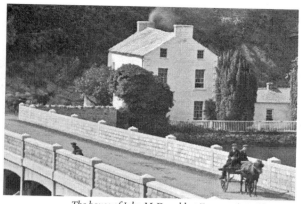

The house of John McDonald at Ferrycarrig Bridge. It was extensively damaged in an assault by an anti-Treaty IRA unit on a Free State garrison that was guarding the bridge. (detail from Lawrence Collection/NLI)

In the early hours of Wednesday, 9 August 1922, on the road from Enniscorthy into Wexford, the tranquillity of Ferrycarrig was shattered just a month after the fighting in Enniscorthy. A garrison of 15 Free State soldiers was based in the home of John McDonald, beside Ferrycarrig Bridge. The troops kept a Lewis machine gun in McDonald's licensed grocery shop (later known as the Oak Tavern).

Just after 3am, shots were fired at two soldiers who were on sentry duty on the bridge. An estimated 70 to 100 anti-Treaty IRA volunteers, under the command of Bob Lambert, were positioned at four commanding points overlooking the location. Sergeant J. Darby, who was in charge of the unit, called off the sentry from the bridge to McDonald's house. There they took up positions with the other troops and returned fire. Shots continued to rain down from Lambert's men, penetrating the windows and door of the house. Sergeant Darby, a native of Westmeath, was hit three times in the arm, leg and hip but continued to direct operations.

The Free State force's machine gun was out of action and they had only rifles and revolvers to respond with. Also inside the house were the housekeeper Mrs Whelan and three lady friends of hers, who were screaming hysterically as they took shelter under their beds. The IRA repeatedly called on the troops, who were vastly outnumbered, to surrender. But they were ignored. Grenades were hurled into the house as the IRA came into closer range and surrounded the property. They threatened to burn the house down.

One of the garrison, Edmond McEvoy, who was in his teens and from Belfast, was mortally wounded. His last words were, *'Jesus Christ, have mercy on me... fight on boys!'*

Sergeant Darby was becoming weaker as the terrified females pleaded with him to surrender. Finally, after two and a half hours of gunfire, a white flag was hoisted. The volunteers cheered and then disarmed the soldiers, removing some of their boots and leggings.

Meanwhile, a simultaneous attack on the military barracks in Wexford town was mounted by the Murrintown IRA. They fired down on the army garrison from positions on Trespan Rock. Nearly 300 years earlier, Cromwell's troops had been positioned on the same outcrop, from where they aimed their artillery on Wexford Castle, which originally stood on the site of the barracks.

Two Free State units went in pursuit of the attackers, taking with them a Lewis machine gun. One proceeded via the Faythe, the other along Distillery Road, with a plan to encircle the IRA. But they made good their retreat. There were no casualties on either side. During the two hours of gunfire, many houses in the vicinity of the barracks were hit. Some residents had miraculous escapes and when day broke, spent cartridges were found in houses on Castlehill Street, Parnell Street, Barrack Street, Lambert Place and King Street.

When the shooting in Ferrycarrig was heard, a party of Free State troops responded. But their journey was impeded by a felled tree that blocked the road to Ferrycarrig and they were forced to detour through adjoining fields. As they approached, they were fired on by two IRA men who were withdrawing from the fighting. When the conflict was over, the men of the flying column cycled off into the night.

The Ferrycarrig casualties were attended by Rev. James Gaul, Barntown. They included four wounded soldiers, all from County Kildare, who were removed to the County Hospital. The remains of Edmond McEvoy was conveyed to the County Infirmary on Hill Street. Sergeant Darby and one other injured soldier were transported by special train the next day to hospital in Dublin.

(sources: The People and Free Press, August 1922)

The military barracks on Barrack Street was attacked as a diversionary tactic. (photo: Des Kiely)

The Liberator's Repeal speech to the people of Wexford

Daniel O'Connell 'monster meeting', from an engraving of a painting by Joseph Patrick Haverty. (NLI)

DANIEL O'CONNELL, the Kerry-born barrister and political activist, held over fifty 'monster meetings' throughout the country in the summer of 1843. The gatherings were the largest recorded in modern Irish history. They were called by O'Connell, 'The Liberator', in support of his campaign to repeal the Act of Union of 1800 between Great Britain and Ireland. Since 1801, Irish Members of Parliament and peers had to take their seats in Westminster, instead of College Green in Dublin. O'Connell wanted an independent Kingdom of Ireland that would govern itself under Queen Victoria.

Having achieved Catholic Emancipation in 1829, O'Connell founded the Repeal Association in 1830. It sought legislative independence for Ireland with full Catholic participation.

The County Wexford public Repeal rally was scheduled for Thursday, 20 July 1843 in the townland of Tomduff, about a mile outside Enniscorthy, in a field off the road to Clonroche – ever since known as the 'Repeal Field'. Daniel O'Connell arrived the night before, accompanied by the youngest of his seven children, Daniel Jnr., and Thomas Steele. His most personally devoted adherent, Steele was known as the 'Head Pacificator' of the Repeal movement. Along the Dublin road, the local clergy and their parishioners cheered O'Connell as he passed in his carriage through towns such as Camolin and Ferns. All three stayed the night in Enniscorthy at the residence of Dr James Keating, the Bishop of Ferns. Notices had been placed around the town requesting people not to shout as they passed, lest The Liberator should be disturbed by the noise.

The mammoth gathering from around the county and beyond attracted vast throngs. The local press reported 300,000 though this number was probably exaggerated. In the early hours of Thursday morning, inhabitants of the baronies of Forth and Bargy marched into Wexford town, where they were joined by its residents. Led by brass bands playing patriotic airs, floats with colours flying and trade bodies, thousands joined the parade on foot or horseback. Some opted to travel up the Slaney in 150 boats. The people of Ross, Gorey, Ferns, Ballygarret, Newtownbarry also marched en masse towards Enniscorthy, led by marching bands. General Thomas Cloney, the 1798 veteran, arrived at the head of a procession numbering seven or eight thousand that included Repealers from Carlow and Kilkenny.

At around 10am, the trade bodies of Enniscorthy, Wexford and Ross assembled near Enniscorthy Castle and proceeded with accompanying bands to the bishop's residence. Having presented an address to O'Connell, The Liberator joined the procession and was paraded through the streets of the town that were lined with cheering crowds of men, women and children. Almost every house was decorated with laurels, flowers and banners bearing slogans such as 'Erin go Brath' and 'Ireland as she shall be – a Nation.'

A platform had been erected in the field and was crowded with special guests when O'Connell arrived to tumultuous cheering. Members of the various trades entered the field with their banners flying, accompanied by uniformed marching bands.

Bishop Keating opened the meeting, saying: *'My dear friends of the county of Wexford ... You have come here quiet, orderly, and peaceable men, such as you always have been, for that is your character ... Is Ireland to remain in vassalage and bondage until the sounding of the last trumpet? ... You have assembled here in vast numbers to petition the Imperial parliament for the Repeal of the Legislative Union, and to give back to Ireland that of which she was cruelly deprived – to restore to her, her domestic parliament ...*

You have the first man in Europe to assist you – you have the Liberator ... We will assist him in a peaceful, legal, and constitutional way. Let us pledge ourselves, one and all, never to abandon that sacred and holy cause until we shall see Ireland as she ought to be:

Great, glorious and free
First flower of earth, first gem of the sea.'

Dr Keating then moved that the chair be taken by John Maher MP of Ballinkeele House, Ballymurn, who made a powerful speech in favour of Repeal. He opened with the well-known lines from the Scottish writer, Sir Walter Scott:

Breathes there a man with soul so dead,
Who never to himself hath said,
This is my own, my native land!

A number of speakers followed, all supporting the reinstatement of the Irish Parliament. They included John Talbot of Ballytrent House and Castle Talbot, Sheppard Jeffares, Mayor of Wexford and Rev Dr John Sinnott, President of St Peter's College.

The Freeman's Journal correspondent who attended wrote: '*I was informed that all the Catholic clergymen of the county were present ... I was glad to perceive that a gentleman was present from The Times, who, I have no doubt, will convey to our rulers, through their favourite organ, a just description of the glorious proceedings of the day.'*

When O'Connell rose to deliver his speech, he was greeted with prolonged applause. '*It has been my fortune to behold assemblages of large masses of my countrymen,'* he began, '*but I never saw so noble an assemblage as the present'*, which elicited enthusiastic cheering from the crowd.

'*Our enemies have exhausted all their threats'*, he said, '*and now they depend upon the silly notion, that we will be tired of asking for our liberties. The fellow who stood above Enniscorthy bridge to wait until the Slaney would run dry that he might walk over dryshod was a wise fellow when compared to the Duke of Wellington, who thinks he has only to stand by a little, and that the Irish people will give up the pursuit of that freedom which is their right, and which they never will relax their efforts to obtain until the parliament is in College Green.'*

O'Connell was a charismatic figure and eloquent orator, one of the most popular of his day. He had a deep, booming voice which he employed to great effect to his vast audience. He could touch the hearts of his listeners, then convulse them with his homely humour.

'Repeal is on the wild winds of heaven. The breeze fresh from Wexford blows over it; that gale is scattering it through Ireland. The seeds of liberty are upon the pinions of that wind, and they shall cover the entire land with the angel wing of protection and freedom,' he declared to loud cheers.

Detail from a portrait of Daniel O'Connell by Limerick artist John Gubbins. It hangs in O'Connell's home, Derrynane House, Co. Kerry. (photo: Des Kiely)

'The House of Lords and the House of Commons have declared against Repeal, and therefore it must be rebellious to seek it. If the Duke of Wellington did not fight better than he reasons, he would be beaten ten times over, despite the bravery of his troops at Waterloo; and if he were not a better general than he is a logician, he would be the greatest dunderhead that ever was at the head of an army,' said O'Connell. Dublin-born Arthur Wellesley, Duke of Wellington, a former Prime Minister, was now leader of the Conservative Party in the House of Lords. Robert Peel was the Conservative Prime Minister.

'From the time that the English first put their feet upon the green soil of Wexford, they never conquered us in battle, or gained anything from us by open fight. They never gained an advantage over us but by deceiving us.' On the payment of tithes [a ten percent tax] to the Protestant Church, he said: *'Why, I ask, should we pay for the support of a religion from which we derive no spiritual advantage?'* He also criticized the Grand Jury Cess [the equivalent of county council rates] and the Poor Rate [local property tax]. On the land question, he denounced the landlords, though in far more moderate terms than would the Land League later in the century.

O'Connell concluded his speech amidst loud cheers: *'Let there then be but one cry through the county of Wexford: Old Ireland and Liberty; Liberty and Old Ireland ...* *We will soon —Protestant and Catholic, Presbyterian and Dissenter — all, all be combined. We are working for all, not for a few. The morning of liberty is dawning upon us, and Old Ireland shall be a nation. The shout of liberty shall be re-echoed from the mountain tops, and the young eagle of Irish freedom shall soar aloft, proclaiming to the nations that it was by virtuous, and virtuous means alone, that Ireland rose to legislative independence.'*

According to *The Freeman's Journal*: *'There were detachments of cavalry and infantry and a large body of police in town, but they remained in their barracks. It is almost needless to say that there was not the slightest necessity for their interference, the most perfect order having marked all the proceedings.'*

The procession regrouped and escorted The Liberator back to the bishop's house. A hundred-foot-long temporary pavilion had been set up for a public banquet in his honour. Chandeliers hung from the roof and it was decorated with evergreens and laurels and a number of banners. Behind the top table hung an image of the Irish House of Parliament with the inscription: *'Our Old House at home – it was and shall be.'* On either side wall, a pair of banners read: *'Catholic Emancipation 1829 – Repeal 1843.'*

The chair for the event was the Repeal Association MP for New Ross, John Talbot. He was married to Anne Redmond, daughter of Walter Redmond, the Wexford banker. Daniel O'Connell sat to his right, along with a dozen other guests. To his left was Bishop Keating and a similar number of special guests. A local band that entertained the guests for the evening was occasionally joined by a harpist who sat behind the chairman. The proceedings were opened with a toast to Queen Victoria to the strains of *God Save the Queen*.

The Liberator rose and was received with loud cheers. He said: *'It will be easily admitted that this day must have been to me one of the most cheering that the sun ever shone upon. I think there is not one of you but must be convinced that a day more rewarding to my struggles for Ireland never yet appeared*

Derrynane House, Co. Kerry, the ancestral home of Daniel O'Connell. (photo: Des Kiely)

during my existence. It was a delightful scene today; it was pleasing to take part in it; it was cheering to behold it. It was animating to perceive its connection with the cause of Irish liberty, and it was promising. It was an anticipation of the future that cannot fail to operate, and produce an active operation for Ireland.'

'Some person said to me that Wexford is late in the contest, Wexford is slow, but Wexford is sure. It was well to let these who may be more flippant in their enthusiasm precede your actual demonstration, but there are none of them that can boast a higher, stronger, nobler sentiment of determination than Wexford this day exhibited. It is strange to say it, but I feel almost overcome.'

He continued: 'My mind is filled with the majestic scene that appeared before me today. I see what a quantity I have of physical force, of moral power, of intellect and physical energy, and of all those elements that lift nations from a prostrate situation and raise them to the station of independent power.'

Believed to be the only surviving photographic image (daguerreotype) of Daniel O'Connell. Taken while he was held in the Richmond Bridewell (now Griffith College) in Dublin in 1844. He is shown wearing his famous green velvet 'Repeal Cap', embroidered with golden shamrocks. (National Gallery of Ireland)

'We also know the state of the peasantry of the country, and is it not time to consider it? It is impossible to conceive that the relation between landlord and tenant should not be altered. The laws are insufferable in their present state, and almost all the mischief is mischief created by acts of parliament that were made by the landlords themselves.'

He concluded: 'We are struggling for the operative classes; we are struggling for the agricultural classes and the peace and tranquillity of the higher order. We are struggling for the liberty and prosperity of Old Ireland, and in the mighty struggle nothing can exceed excitation of mind with which I hail the accession of the men of Wexford, and pledge myself to all Ireland, in your names, that I never will give up the struggle until the parliament is in College Green.'

O'Connell announced in Enniscorthy his plans to hold similar monster meetings in Tuam, Castlebar and on 15 August at the Hill of Tara in County Meath. This was symbolic, being the historic seat of the High Kings of Ireland. An estimated 750,000 people thronged to the venue for up to three days in advance. This was by far his biggest rally. *The Illustrated London News* reported that *'the procession from Dunshaughlin, which conducted Mr. O'Connell, fully occupied a mile of road.'* The sheer scale of the gathering, however, made the authorities uneasy. When his next rally was announced for Clontarf the Prime Minister, Robert Peel, issued a ban at the last moment. Fearing rebellion from such huge numbers that The Liberator's meetings were attracting, armed militia ringed the venue in Clontarf. O'Connell feared bloodshed and backed down. He sent word that people heading to Clontarf were to turn back. This spelt disaster for The Liberator, who would never recover from the humiliation.

O'Connell was arrested and charged with 'conspiring to change the constitution by illegal methods.' Following a lengthy trial, he, along with a number of allies, was sentenced to a year's imprisonment. They were allowed to choose their own place of detention and opted for the Richmond Bridewell. However, they never served out their sentences in prison cells, but in comfort in the homes of the Governor and Deputy Governor. Although hailed a martyr, O'Connell's incarceration became known as the 'Richmond Picnic.' His conviction was deemed unjust by the House of Lords, and they quashed it. He was freed after serving only three months. On his release, he was paraded in triumph through Dublin on a gilded chariot.

With his health failing and approaching seventy years of age, he continued to campaign but had now lost the power to influence matters in London. While Famine raged in Ireland, he made his final plea in Westminster in 1847 for help for the starving, but was refused. On his way to Rome on pilgrimage three months later, he died in Genoa. His parting words to his physician were:

The National Bank building (right) on Custom House Quay, Wexford. O'Connell was appointed its first governor. (NLI)

'My body to Ireland, my heart to Rome, and my soul to heaven.' His heart was taken to the church of Sant'Agata dei Goti in Rome and his body to Dublin. But since the 1920s his heart has been missing and its whereabouts remains a mystery.

A partial repeal of the Act of Union that he had sought through peaceful means would not be achieved until 1922, following rebellion and armed struggle.

Mysterious mini tsunami that hit Kilmore Quay in 1854

Kilmore Quay in the 1800s. Some of these thatched cottages have been standing for over two centuries.

WILLIAM CAMPBELL, known locally as the Diver, was working on the building of the new pier in Kilmore Quay on the evening of 16 September 1854. It would replace a makeshift one built of loose rocks by local fishermen that dated to the late 1780s. This was the first proper quay to be constructed in Kilmore Quay. William was in one of four boats employed in the construction work. While fetching an implement and facing away from the sea, he *'heard a mighty rush of water against the back of the pier, and in a moment came sweeping around the pier head, full three feet high and abreast,'* he told the *Wexford Independent*.

William said this 'extraordinary phenomenon' occurred an hour and thirty minutes following low tide. The shoreline was dry and crowded with small sailing craft. Within five minutes every boat was afloat on a high tide. The water receded again five minutes later to an extremely low spring tide. This occurrence repeated itself seven times in the course of two and a half hours.

To the east, St Patrick's Bridge, a causeway of rock and shingle that extends towards Little Saltee Island, remained dry. But what Campbell described as a cascade was formed from end to end, though the sea was not rough. The legend of St Patrick's Bridge goes that our patron saint, while chasing the Devil out of Ireland, hurled rocks at him as he headed out to sea and these formed the bridge.

William recalled: *'Standing on the top of the parapet wall of the pier, I could descry two different currents running parallel, and counter currents to these quite visible, the discoloured water running east at a rate of ten or twelve miles an hour, and the intervening water, of the original green hue, as is stationary. These tide currents were as far as the shore of the Saltee Islands. I can only compare the current to the opening of a sluice gate.'*

None of the boats tied up near the shore was damaged apart from a few becoming untethered and being pushed aground. Had the occurrence taken place during high tide, this low-lying district would have been submerged, resulting in great losses. In the *Belfast Newsletter* account of the event, it was noted that: *'It was a fortunate matter that the event happened late in the day, as, had it occurred in the morning, the many bathers who frequent the bathing-places on the coast must inevitably have been drowned.'*

The newspaper speculated that this phenomenon may have been caused by an earthquake in some distant land. It was remembered that there had been a similar occurrence in the area almost hundred years previously on the day after the Lisbon earthquake of 1 November 1755. That event was one of the deadliest earthquakes in history. It almost totally destroyed the city, lying due south of Ireland, and resulted in between 30,000 and 40,000 deaths in Lisbon alone. Approximately forty minutes after the earthquake, a tsunami flooded the city as well as towns along the Algarve coast. A firestorm in Lisbon was started by candles – lit in homes and churches all around the city for All Saints' Day – being knocked over and asphyxiating thousands of its citizens. The tsunami also destroyed towns in North Africa, on the Andalusian coast of Spain and ports on the islands of Madeira and the Azores. Shocks were felt as far north as Finland. Tsunamis as high as 20 metres struck Martinique

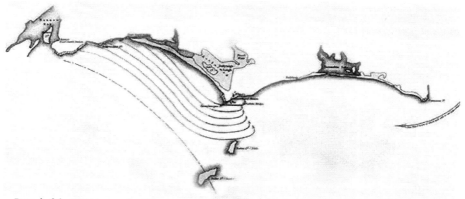

Record of the 1854 tsunami at Kilmore Quay, from the 'Earthquake Catalogue' by R. & J. Mallet, 1858.

and Barbados on the other side of the Atlantic. The Spanish Arch in Galway city was partially destroyed and Kinsale was flooded. Aughinish Island in County Clare was created when a low-lying connection to the mainland was washed away.

The Irish geophysicist Robert Mallet.

But strangely no earthquake was recorded in the Atlantic on that date in 1854. There were no reports elsewhere of such an occurrence as described by William Campbell on the south coast of Ireland. In the *Earthquake Catalogue*, published in two volumes by the British Association for the Advancement of Science in 1858, the event was recorded and described, along with a map, as a probable tsunami. The catalogue was produced by Robert Mallet and his son John, who was then Professor of Chemistry at the University of Alabama.

Robert Mallet, born in Dublin in 1810, was a renowned geophysicist, civil engineer and inventor. He and his son John carried out landmark experiments on Killiney Beach and Dalkey Island in 1849 and 1850 respectively. They buried kegs of gunpowder in the sand, detonated them and measured how long it took the shock waves to travel over a set distance. They proved that the speed of sound differs in rock and in sand. These experiments laid the foundations for the modern science of studying earthquakes and Robert is regarded as the founder of the science of seismology. A plaque on Killiney beach commemorates Mallet's study.

Just a month before the *Wexford Independent* carried the story of the mini tsunami under the headline 'Extraordinary Phenomenon', they published a letter to the editor describing how the same William Campbell, *'better known by the name of the talented Diver'*, removed two of the most dangerous rocks that stood directly in line with the entrance to the pier, posing a danger to fishing boats. They were known as the 'Great Ling' and the 'Big Shane'. The Diver and his son, who had earlier bored through the rocks, then set explosive charges within. *'The fuse being ignited, we took our departure to a civil distance, and almost immediately a grand explosion took place. We went to see the result and to my astonishment this huge mass of rock was divided into four quarters, as even as one would cut a griddle cake, completely through, leaving an opening between each quarter of at least nine inches; rendering it an easy matter to raise and carry them away, to any place*

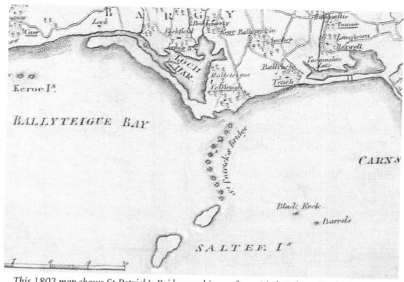

This 1802 map shows St Patrick's Bridge reaching as far as Little Saltee Island. The pier and village of Kilmore Quay had not yet been built. Most of Ballyteige Lough (left of centre) was reclaimed as part of a Famine relief scheme in the 1840s.

they may be required', wrote 'A Constant Reader and Real Friend of Progress'.

Kilmore Quay's history goes back to the 1700s and no further than about 300 years. The village was established close to Crossfarnoge Point, known locally as Forlorn Point, about three miles south of Kilmore. Lucrative fishing grounds off the Saltee Islands were what attracted small beach-launched boats

The 15th century Ballyteige Castle is now part of a working farm. (photo: Des Kiely)

to the area. However, the seashore was very exposed, offering no shelter in poor weather. The Kilmore fishermen undertook to build a pier in the 1780s to moor their boats. They removed rocks from the shoreline, floated them out on rafts and piled them on one another. A village slowly developed around the harbour and a lifeboat was installed in 1847. A more suitable quay was constructed in the 1850s, creating a much safer harbour. This attracted larger fishing boats as well as schooners that imported coal and exported potatoes. St Peter's Church was built in 1875. The harbour was extended and deepened in the mid-1990s with a 55-berth marina added.

The waters can be treacherous off this stretch of coastline from Hook Head to Carnsore Point. With its low-lying land profile, hundreds of sailing ships foundered in poor visibility over the centuries. A memorial garden overlooking the sea was established in 2001 to remember all those lost at sea.

The four-storey Ballyteige Castle was erected by the Anglo-Norman colonist family, the Whittys, in the 15th century. This is one of the finest examples of a tower house in the county and is part of a working farm, sited off the road from Kilmore Quay to Baldwinstown. The earliest record of the family shows Robert Wythay [sic] at Ballyteige in 1247. The original Ballyteige Castle was attacked and burned by the Kavanaghs in 1408 and this was its replacement. The Kavanaghs (Uí Cheinnselaig) retained the kingship of Leinster up to 1603. The Whittys also occupied Dungulph Castle near Fethard, built in 1330 by Adam Whitty. Following the Cromwellian invasion of 1649-50, Ballyteige Castle was granted to the Colcloughs of Tintern. John Henry Colclough resided there in 1798 and was a leading member of the United Irishmen. Along with his wife and Beauchamp Bagenal Harvey of Bargy Castle, he was arrested while they hid in a cave on the Saltee Islands. They were planning to escape to France but were betrayed, and both Colclough and Harvey were hanged on Wexford Bridge.

Ballyhealy Castle, built by the Whittys, passed to the Cheevers and later the Bunburys. (photo: Tony Crosbie)

Ballyhealy Castle, about a mile south-east of Kilmore village, is believed to have been built by Sir Richard Whitty. This 15th century tower house passed to the Cheevers family, perhaps through marriage. The Flemish Cheevers (or Chièvres) also arrived with the Anglo-Normans. They held Danescastle and Killiane Castle, south of Wexford town. Ballyhealy and Killiane also fell victim to the Cromwellian confiscations and were granted to Colonel Bunbury, a Cromwellian soldier.

'Tottenham in his Boots' and the critical Parliamentary vote

Charles Tottenham standing on the steps of the Irish House of Commons. This print, from a painting known as 'Tottenham in his Boots' by Dublin portrait artist Justin Stevens, was published in 1749.

CHARLES TOTTENHAM, a member of the Irish Parliament, is said to have ridden nearly 100 miles through the night from his home, Tottenham Green near Taghmon, to the House of Commons in Dublin to cast his vote in 1731. Rushing into the House in his riding boots and splashed with mud up to his shoulders, Tottenham's casting vote turned the balance against the Government by a majority of one. Although he had the right to enter, he was liable to a hefty penalty of £500, which the rules prescribed for not attending in full dress. He paid the fine. The event made him popular throughout the country and he was toasted by Irish patriots as 'Tottenham in his Boots'.

Charles Tottenham, born in 1685 to Edward Tottenham and Elizabeth (née Hayman), married Ellinor Cliffe of Mulrankin in 1712. Their grand-daughter, Anne Tottenham, was at the centre of the Legend of Loftus Hall in about 1760, when she was about 16 years old and was said to have been visited by the Devil (see story in *Fascinating Wexford History, Volume Two*).

In power at the time were the so-called 'country party' — a coalition of Tories and disaffected Whigs, who claimed to be non-partisan and fighting for the interest of the whole country. An important constitutional question was being debated in the Irish House of Commons between the government and opposition, and a vote on it was imminent. The matter related to whether a sum of £60,000 should go to the King, George II, or remain in the country. This was the amount held in the Irish Treasury, being the balance remaining after paying the interest and principal of the National Debt. The opposition insisted that it should be carried over in the usual constitutional manner from session to session. The government coalition proposed a compromise to entrust it to the King for twenty-one years, and this proposition was put to the vote. The members seemed to be split equally on the matter.

Charles Tottenham, representing New Ross for the Tory party, arrived 'undressed', in dirty boots and riding attire and covered with mud, having just ridden from County Wexford. He rushed into the chamber without washing or changing his clothes. In the 1700s, strict formal dress was the rule and included the fashion of wearing a wig. The Sergeant-at-Arms, who was responsible for keeping order in the House, endeavoured to bar his entrance and warned the chamber that a member wanted to force his way into the

Charles Tottenham was MP for New Ross from 1727 to 1758.

House. The Speaker, Sir Ralph Gore, decided that he had no power to exclude Tottenham and felt obliged to admit him just at the critical moment. Tottenham strode into the chamber as the division was just about to be taken and cast his vote, which resulted in the money being kept in the country. Versions of the story say that he rode from Ballycarney, near Ferns, where he had property, or even from Loftus Hall but the anecdote of 'Tottenham in his Boots' was recounted for years after.

Charles Tottenham was made a Freeman of

Tottenham Green near Taghmon, home of Charles Tottenham, was built in 1712 and demolished in 1950.
(photo courtesy Frank Doyle)

New Ross in 1711 and represented the constituency in the Irish House of Commons from 1727 until shortly before his death in 1758. He was also High Sheriff of Wexford in 1737-38 and Mayor of Wexford in 1739. Charles and Ellinor Tottenham had six sons, including John and Charles, both of whom became MPs for New Ross, and two daughters. When Ellinor died in 1745 he married Mary, daughter of John Grogan of Johnstown Castle, the following year. Mary was the widow of Andrew Knox of Rathmacknee Castle and later, William Hore of Harperstown.

In the period 1727 to 1760, the Irish House of Commons had 300 members sitting at each session. It was dominated by the Protestant elite since an Act of 1691 required all members to take oaths of allegiance and supremacy. Catholics were barred from voting under the Penal Laws, imposed in an attempt to force Catholics to accept the established Church of Ireland. However, wealthy Catholics could vote in the Irish House of Commons elections and hold seats in the Irish House of Lords. Elections were held only at the start of the reign of a new monarch. In the general election for the first parliament in the reign of George II in 1727, the Disenfranchising Act was passed by the Parliament of Ireland and came into effect in 1728, prohibiting all Catholics from voting and so putting further pressure on Catholics to conform to the Established Church.

It was not until 1793 that all males, irrespective of religion, holding a freehold property with a rental value of at least £2 annually, the so-called 'forty-shilling freeholders', were permitted to vote. The forty-shilling freehold was established by the Act of 1542 and many candidates fraudulently created freeholders in order to increase votes. Catholics were barred from membership of the parliament and this was enforced until 1829. The qualification to vote was raised to a rental value of £10 with the passing of the Catholic Relief Act of 1829, thereby excluding many previous voters, both Catholic and Protestant.

The county of Wexford was represented in the Irish Parliament by nine constituencies: Bannow, Clonmines, Enniscorthy, Fethard, Gorey, New Ross, Taghmon, Wexford Borough and Wexford County. Two of these, the 'rotten boroughs' of Bannow (without a single inhabited house) and Clonmines (with one solitary house), continued to be represented each by two Members until the Act of Union in 1800, when Ireland became part of the United Kingdom. Seats were bought and sold and £2,000 was being paid by the mid-1700s. In the general election in 1727, Charles Tottenham was returned for New Ross. Bannow was represented by Samuel Boyse and George Ogle and Clonmines by Thomas Loftus and Edward Corker.

The election of county members was held in county courts specially convened by the sheriffs. The appointment of sheriffs was influenced by the landlords, who were now seeking election. The sheriff could influence the return of a member, sometimes even arresting voters who favoured an opposition candidate. Votes were often bought and pressure put on voters by the candidates. Voting was extremely slow and in public in the presence of the candidates and their agents, who debated the voters' qualifications and insisted on the administering of oaths. In the general election of 1754, voting in County Wexford took place over thirteen days. Prior to 1793, few counties in Ireland had more than a thousand voters.

After three months of fighting in Wexford during the rebellion of 1798, many rebels went into hiding for years after and stability took several years to return to the county. The British Government now called for the abolition of the Irish Parliament and for Ireland to be ruled directly from London and brought under tighter British control. The proposed union met with strong resistance in the Irish Parliament of course, where seats were regarded as property and borough compensation was demanded. Through bribery and the payment of compensation, even for the loss of 'rotten boroughs' such as

Bannow and Clonmines, the Act of Union was passed in 1800. Ireland was to be represented at the Parliament in Westminster by 100 members in the House of Commons and the monarch was now known as the King (or Queen) of the United Kingdom of Great Britain and Ireland. The union remained until the recognition of the Irish Free State and the signing of the Anglo-Irish Treaty in 1921.

PARLIAMENT HOUSE, DUBLIN

At the time of Tottenham's nighttime ride from Wexford to Dublin in 1731, the Irish Parliament was sitting in temporary accommodation in The King's Hospital, then located in Queen Street, between 1729 and 1739. Chichester House on Hoggen Green (later College Green) was the home of the Irish Parliament since 1661. Before then, the parliament met in Dublin Castle and in the 15th century in Christchurch Cathedral.

Chichester House was in a delapidated state and in 1729 work began on a new purpose-built Irish House of Parliament building on the same site. It was designed by Edward Pearce, who deliberately filled in the windows with brick to avoid the Window Tax of the time. By the 1780s more space was needed and the renowned architect James Gandon was commissioned to make alterations. The semi-circular building served as Ireland's Parliament until the Act of Union in 1800. The building was purchased by the Bank of Ireland in 1803.

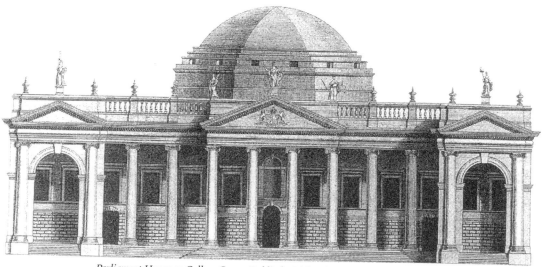

Parliament House on College Green, Dublin by Irish painter and engraver Peter Mazell, 1767.
The original domed House of Commons chamber was destroyed in a fire in the 1790s.

Wexford cargo ship plundered by wreckers on Merseyside

A schooner similar to the Mary & Betsey that ran into a severe gale en route to Liverpool.

THE WRITER Amyas Griffith noted in the late 1700s that Wexford's chief export was corn and other agricultural produce and trade at the time was chiefly with Bristol, Milford and Liverpool. By the turn of the century, Wexford was the sixth busiest port in Ireland and the quays were lined with cargo ships. The Ballast Bank was constructed in 1832, from where visiting ships could load and unload gravel or sand to ensure stability. But land reclamation during the Famine years ultimately resulted in the shallow harbour silting up, making access to shipping difficult.

Before this decline in maritime trading activity, one of the many cargo vessels operating out of Wexford Harbour was the *Mary & Betsey*. Under Captain Thomas Lambert, with a crew of six and carrying four passengers, the wooden brig of 180 tons burden, set sail out of Wexford bound for Liverpool on 24 October 1820. On board was a cargo of corn, pigs and sheep. Only three of the crewmen would survive the voyage.

In Liverpool Bay, the Wirral Peninsula, which is bounded by the River Mersey, the Irish Sea and the River Dee, had dangerous sandbanks lying off its coast that posed great danger to shipping. In the early 1800s this stretch of shoreline was notorious for its wreckers. They would lure Liverpool-bound vessels onto the sandbanks using decoy lights and flares. When the ships ran aground, the wreckers plundered them, robbing their cargoes and showing little or no mercy towards the crew and passengers. Some wrecking, however, was not deliberate. Many ships caught up in winter storms were blown onto the banks. Local people would soon arrive on the scene and salvage what they could.

Because of these sandbanks located off the Leasowe Coast near the entrance to the Mersey estuary, a number of pilots cruised in sailing boats and boarded approaching ships. These pilots took charge of navigating the vessels safely through the hazardous channels towards Liverpool. As the *Mary & Betsey* made her approach on the morning after leaving Wexford, she took on board a local pilot at around eleven o'clock.

A strong wind was brewing by two o'clock and an hour later the men adjusted the foresail, making the ship 'heave to', in order to slow its forward progress. By four o'clock the wind picked up and two hours later, as darkness fell, the vessel first struck the Mockbeggar Bank off Wallasey and was soon blown towards the shore.

Crewman Edward Campbell later recalled: '*We then let go the best bower anchor, from the starboard side, and gave her the whole length of the cable, yet she would not fetch up, but beat very heavily against the bottom. The pilot then ordered us to cut, and loose the foresail, that she might be prevented from sinking so heavily, by being pressed down by the sail.*'

Wexford quays bustling with cargo ships in the late 19th century. (photo: NLI)

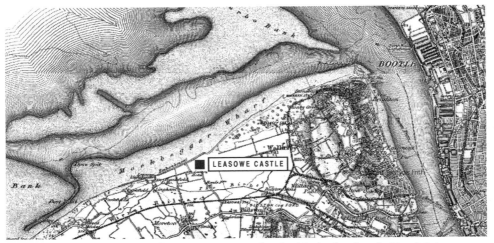

The treacherous sandbanks off the Leasowe Coast on the Wirral Peninsula, where the Mary & Betsey ran aground on its approach to the River Mersey and port of Liverpool (right).

But their endeavours were in vain and all hands on board agreed to take to the longboat. With the ship lying broadside, the men managed to get the boat over the side. But suddenly, a rolling surge smashed against it. Unaware of the damage it had caused, the men got into the boat, which immediately began to sink. However, the longboat had not unhooked from the ship's tackle and was still attached by ropes. The men struggled to make their way back out. Six of them clung to the fore ropes and the pilot to the main rigging. But the captain and two of the passengers were lost.

The men cut away the foresail and topsail to lighten the effect of the gale-force wind. But they were being battered by the sea swell and found it difficult to hold on. One of the passengers, John Leary, a butcher from Wexford, was unable to maintain his grip and fell into the water below and drowned.

Another young passenger, James Pierce from Rathaspeck, had been standing on the main boom and holding onto the mast. The next swell knocked the ship onto her side and into the sand. The sea rose over the ship's hull and the pilot grabbed hold of the young man but was washed away and was lost. Another man, who had been holding onto the second mast and then a rope, grew weak and had to let go. He too perished in the darkness.

The sea surge came right over the *Mary & Betsey* as she lay broadside. The ship's mate, Patrick Welsh, was still hanging precariously to the top mast as it lay horizonal high above the water. He was exhausted by now and about to fall. The rest of the men pulled him up by rope with great difficulty. With four men now hanging on the rigging, they decided to hold onto one another; if they were to drown, they would go down together. As the sea washed over them they held tight and just had time to draw breath between each swell. The men held on in the darkness for about four hours until finally the tide changed and the water level began to subside.

Patrick Welsh remained on the rigging with one of the crew, Edward Cullen, while the other two crewmen, Edward Campbell and Paul Swainson, crawled down to join the pilot who had sat alone on the forechains of the vessel. They could soon hear dogs barking along the shore as morning broke and a sailing boat appeared. The crew of the vessel called out for the men on the stricken *Mary & Betsey* to climb aboard. Campbell and Swainson made their way into the boat but Cullen and Welsh, who by now was only semi-conscious, remained hanging onto the rigging.

Edward Campbell later told the *Liverpool Mercury* following the incident: *'When I looked down from the rigging there was a great crowd of people (more than a hundred) with horses and carts. It was just at break of day...'* He believed these were plunderers, there to steal what they could get their hands on. When the same boat returned, the men on board called this time to Edward Cullen and Patrick Welsh to climb down. After much persuasion, Cullen apprehensively joined them, not knowing what his fate might be in the hands of the strangers. He was transferred to a cart and taken to safety above the high-water mark. The two men returned and convinced the mate, Patrick Welsh, who was by now delirious and suffering from fatigue, to also come down.

Meanwhile, the *Mary & Betsey* was being plundered of its cargo and the personal belongings of the crew and passengers. The vessel was completely stripped by the wreckers, leaving nothing but the standing rigging and masts. Horse-drawn carts, some laden with corn and others with whatever else could be plundered from the ship, hurriedly made off in all directions into the countryside. They left a number of corpses lying where they had washed up on the sand. Dead pigs and sheep also lay scattered along the shore but some were still alive and these were removed on carts. The pilot appears to have saved himself from the wreckage.

The only two locals to show any humanity to the survivors of the tragedy were the two men who took the four crewmen to safety and away from the mob. They were Matthew Shadrick and Robert Atkinson, both carpenters from

Liverpool. The pair were employed by and lodged in nearby Leasowe Castle, where they moved the survivors into the care of its owner, Mrs Margaret Boode and her servants. Campbell, Cullen, Swainson and Welsh were given bedding and wrapped in layers of warm blankets. Edward Cullen recounted later: *'The carpenters called the steward out of bed; and got some rum which they gave to them in small quantities, as they could bear it, and treated them with every kindness. And we firmly believe, and wish it to be mentioned, that if it had not been for the exertions of these good people, we would all have died.'* He continued: *'The carpenters afterwards told me, that in going down to save any of the rest they might find – they saw a corpse lying on the strand; there was a cart passing close by; they asked the people to take it in the cart, but they refused; they went further and saw a bag of potatoes which they took into the cart, but they still refused to take the corpse.'*

Margaret Boode had a reputation in the area for helping shipwrecked sailors, many of whom were lured onto the dangerous sandbanks in the area by plunderers known as the 'Wallasey wreckers'. Many seamen were killed for their jewellery or sometimes just for their clothes. Mrs Boode, the daughter of Liverpool rector Reverend Thomas Dannett, was well known for her charity work and promoting Christianity within the community. The 46-year-old lady feared no one and was renowned for the kindness she showed to strangers. She was the widow of Lewis Boode, a plantation owner in the West Indies. In 1802, she purchased Mockbeggar Hall, built in 1593 for the Earl of Derby. Known as the 'stately pile above the sands', the mansion overlooked the Leasowe Coast. Margaret made many additions to the dwelling and renamed it Leasowe Castle. Six years after the *Mary & Betsey* tragedy, she was travelling by horse and carriage when the horse shied and she was thrown from the coach and killed instantly. As a mark of respect, a large limestone obelisk

Leasowe Castle, home of Margaret Boode, where the surviving seamen were cared for.

was erected at the spot. Unfortunately the ship's mate, Patrick Welsh, did not survive the ordeal and died a short time after being taken to Leasowe Castle. His remains were brought to Liverpool and interred at the expense of

The Margaret Boode Memorial in Wallasey, late 1800s.

a Mr Murphy, the proprietor of the Hibernian Hotel. The others who perished were: the captain, Thomas Lambert, and crewmen Nicholas Doyle and William Kennedy. The four passengers who also drowned were: James Pierce of Rathaspeck, Philip Welsh from Piercestown and James Welsh and John Leary, both from Wexford town. All were buried in Wallasey Churchyard, paid for by Wexford natives residing in Liverpool. On 4 November, the hull was refloated and taken to Liverpool.

When the authorities arrived on the scene one wrecker informed on the other and thus much of the plunder was restored. At a court case that followed in Chester, Thomas Moore, a local labourer, was convicted of stealing ropes from the wreck of the *Mary & Betsey* and sentenced to death. Under the headline *'Affecting and Disgraceful Narrative'*, the local newspaper concluded: *'It is hoped, that all those persons who have hitherto looked upon wrecking as a lawful trade, will learn from the sentence, that, by the law of the land, as well as the laws of humanity, it is considered a most atrocious crime...plundering a vessel in distress (whether wreck or no wreck) is felony without benefit of clergy.'*

By the 18th century, entire communities along the north coast of the Wirral were dependent on wrecking and smuggling. The operation centre in Wallasey was the notorious coastal tavern, Mother Redcap's, which dated back to 1595. Its owner had been the mother of a renowned pirate known as 'Redcap'. Contraband goods were concealed here and transported inland through secret tunnels. In 1690, William of Orange had his troops camped on the Leasowe Coast, awaiting ships to take them to Ireland, culminating in the Battle of the Boyne. Mother Redcap's is said to have been used to convey despatches to the troops but that Redcap herself relayed messages from the deposed King James's supporters to many Catholic families living in the Liverpool area.

Great Island – once the site of a major monastic settlement

Early Christian-era settlement reconstructed at the Irish National Heritage Park, Wexford. (photo: Des Kiely)

GREAT ISLAND is a former 600-acre island located in the Waterford Estuary where the Barrow, Suir and Pill (or Campile) rivers meet. Land between the eastern side and the County Wexford mainland was reclaimed in the 1800s and is now farmland. At Kilmokea, on the northern end of the island, there once stood an important 1,500-year-old enclosed ecclesiastic settlement, dating back to the 6th century.

There is an old Celtic legend that tells the story of Cessair, a granddaughter of Noah who escaped the Flood, and arrived at Cumar na dTrí Uiscí – the confluence of the three sister rivers: the Nore, the Barrow and the Suir – the estuary off Great Island. Cessair brought with her three men and 49 maidens and these were supposedly the first people to inhabit the country.

Christianity reached Ireland by the early 5th century and a strategic ecclesiastic enclosure was established on Great Island in the 6th century. The buildings would have been timber structures and none of these survive. A church was also founded here and called after saints Finbarr and Barrfhin and named Kilmokea (*Cill Mac Aodh,* meaning 'Church of the Sons of Hugh'). It is believed that Kilmokea was an important education centre when the monastery was headed by the abbot Suadbhar. There are no stone remains of the ancient settlement apart from the graveyard alongside the ferry road, which contains three fonts and a tiny high cross measuring just 22 inches in height, said to be the smallest in Ireland, and the base of a second high cross.

The small 6th-century high cross at Kilmokea graveyard.

A ferry across the Barrow river to County Kilkenny linked the ancient kingdoms of Osraighe (Ossory) and Uí Ceinnselaig (Kinsella). The road to the ferry ran through the early medieval monastic enclosure at Kilmokea, making it an important and powerful location at the time.

The first recorded Viking raids in Ireland took place on Lambay Island and Rathlin Island in AD 795. The invaders later moved westward, where they attacked monasteries in AD 807. Further Viking raids are recorded on the south coast, with Kilmokea first plundered in AD 822. The Viking Amlaíb Cuarán, King of Dublin, also sacked the Great Island monastery in AD 953 and two further attacks were recorded.

The Frenchman Hervé de Montmorency led the first Anglo-Norman force to arrive in Ireland in 1169, landing at nearby Bannow Bay. Along with Robert FitzStephen, he had come to the aid of the dispossessed King of Leinster, Diarmait Mac Murchada. De Montmorency was an uncle of Richard de Clare (Strongbow), who landed the following year at Passage East. In return, Mac Murchada had promised FitzStephen control of Wexford town and the baronies of Forth and Bargy. Hervé de Montmorency was granted the barony of Shelburne, including Great Island, where he based his headquarters and it became known as Hervey's Island. De Montmorency established a town on the island, speculated to have been close to the Kilmokea enclosure. The town, however, did not survive as a trading port as it needed to compete with both Waterford and William Marshal's town of New Ross.

Strongbow, now Lord of Leinster, instructed De Montmorency to have a Cistercian abbey built on his lands in County Wexford. The result was the construction of Dunbrody Abbey on the banks of the Campile River. The site was named the Port of St. Mary of Dunbrody and the abbey was completed around 1220. After Strongbow died in Dublin in 1176, Hervé de Montmorency granted St. Mary's Church and Bannow Island as well as other churches and lands to Christ Church, Canterbury, where he became a Benedictine monk for a time. Hervé de Montmorency was Dunbrody's first abbot and is said to have died there in 1205, aged 75, and ownership of Great Island then passed to William Marshal.

In the mid-1300s the Black Death had unleashed a devastating wave of death and destruction in the area, having first arrived in the country through ports such as New Ross. In the 1400s a leper colony was established on Great Island to quarantine those stricken by the disease.

The Church of Ireland church at Whitechurch, on the mainland and some three miles from Kilmokea, was constructed in 1740. A house for the rector, Reverend Cubit, was begun in 1794 on the site of the ancient monastery, but through interruptions during the 1798 rebellion it was not completed until 1802 and was named 'Patterdale'. Reverend Thomas Handcock was the next resident and the Ecclesiastical Report to Parliament in 1807 stated that '*the Incumbent Rev Thos Handcock has cure of souls, resides in the neighbour-hood of*

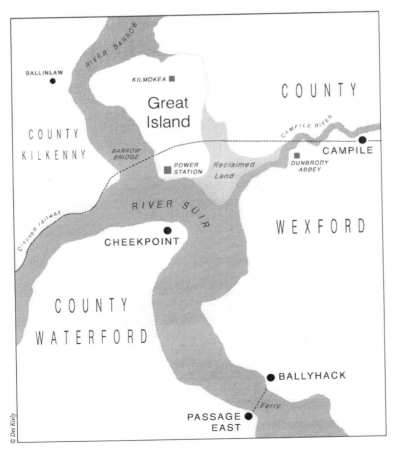

Kilmokea Country Manor is a 200-year-old former rectory at the north end of Great Island. (photo: Des Kiely)

his parish at Ress (Ross), is building a Glebe House, duties discharged by himself.' Reverend Handcock resided at Kilmokea for the next forty years and was followed by Reverends Millar, Robinson, Moore and Greer. The Church of Ireland then sold the house and land to Mrs Isobel Smith in 1937.

Kilmokea House was in a run-down state when it was purchased ten years later in 1947 by Colonel David Price, an ex-British army officer, and his Scottish-born wife Joan. Together they restored and extended the house and developed the magnificent seven-acre gardens with hundreds of different species of plants, between 1950 and the mid-1980s. It was at one of Colonel Price's garden parties at Kilmokea that he, along with Dr Tom Walsh and friends, discussed the idea of holding an opera festival in Wexford. The result was the first Wexford Festival Opera in 1951 in the Theatre Royal. It continues to be held each year in what is now the National Opera House and is one of the world's leading opera festivals.

The property was sold in 1997 to Mark Hewlett and his wife Emma, herself a rector's daughter, who opened the house and gardens to the public the following year. They have continued the restoration work on the house and have extended and enhanced the spectacular gardens. Kilmokea Country Manor & Gardens welcomes guests and even boasts an indoor heated pool, jacuzzi, sauna and gym.

In the 1800s, when the channel at Campile silted up and tidal land between the east of the island and mainland County Wexford was reclaimed as farmland, Great Island began to lose its insular character.

The great engineer Brunel, who died in 1849, had plans to create a railway-connected steamship route between Fishguard and Rosslare. The plan included building a direct railway link between Rosslare and Cork. The construction of Rosslare Harbour and Fishguard Harbour was finally realized by the Fishguard & Rosslare Railways & Harbours Company and both were completed in 1906. The line was to run via Campile and Great Island and on to Waterford, and would involve the construction of two major bridges to cross the rivers Barrow and Suir.

The bridge spanning the Barrow, the longest railway bridge in Ireland at 650 metres long, was designed by the English civil engineer Benjamin Baker and was also completed in 1906. The single-track steel railway bridge links County Wexford at Great Island and County Kilkenny. Two spans close to the Kilkenny side are pivoted to allow ships access to and from New Ross. The railway between Rosslare and Waterford remains in the joint ownership of Irish Rail and Stena Line, but was closed to passenger traffic in 2010. The Rose Fitzgerald Kennedy Bridge, just 9 km upriver, was completed in 2020 and is Ireland's longest road bridge at 887 metres.

The ferry across the Barrow linked Great Island and Ballinlaw, County Kilkenny and probably existed in some form since Early Christian times. The crossing on the river bend was an important one on the Wexford to Waterford route that passed through the monastic settlement. The opening of the Barrow Bridge in 1906 impacted on the ferry operation although a service continued to run until the 1960s. Sample prices for using the ferry crossing were (d=penny): ½d for every man and woman, 1d for every horse, cow or bullock, ¼d for every sheep or goat, ¼d for every stone of wool and ½d for each barrel of corn.

The Barrow Bridge, the longest railway bridge in Ireland, links Great Island and Co. Kilkenny. (photo: Des Kiely)

An early photograph of Great Island Generating Station before the addition of the second chimney in 1972. (photo: ESB archives)

Construction of the ESB's oil-fired Great Island Generating Station got underway in 1963 on a 170-acre site at the southern end of the island and opened in 1967. The facility was the first to be built outside the urban centres of Dublin and Cork. A deep-water jetty was constructed, from where tankers unloaded crude oil to its five storage tanks, each with a capacity to hold 17,000 tonnes of oil. A second 450-feet-high chimney was added in 1972 and by now the station was supplying 20% of Ireland's electricity. The station had a huge visual impact on the landscape, especially when viewed from the County Waterford fishing village of Cheekpoint on the opposite shore. The plant emitted air and noise pollution and also affected local salmon driftnet fishing.

The station was sold to the Spanish utility company Endesa in 2009 and decommissioned the following year. They began construction work in 2012 to change the facility to natural gas. A new carbon steel chimney was built, which is less than half the size of the old concrete affairs. At an early stage the project was sold to SSE Airtricity, who by 2015 were generating energy commercially. The first chimney stacks, built over 50 years ago, were seen as engineering marvels of their time but their demolition would be extremely costly and difficult to dismantle and so they remain standing proudly next to the new gas-fired station.

Wexford Courthouse: gutted in an IRA attack in 1921

Wexford Courthouse, built in 1808, stood directly facing the old wooden Wexford Bridge.

IN HIS ACCOUNT of a visit to Wexford town in 1764, the writer Amyas Griffith wrote: *"In the midst or heart of the Main Street is the bull-ring, where the Court-House, with an excellent clock, &c., stands..."* The courthouse was replaced in 1794 with the construction of the Tholsel. The local municipal building or town hall in Irish towns and cities was known as a *tholsel*; in England as a *tolsey* and in Scotland as the *tolbooth*, where tolls and taxes were collected. Wexford's Tholsel stood in the Bullring (now the location of Stone Solicitors) and housed the mayor and town clerk. Corporation meetings were held on the upper floor and this is where the Court of Conscience, for the recovery of debts, also sat. Later known as the Market House, the Tholsel had five arches at street level, behind which was sited the fish market. The nearby

Corn Market House (now Wexford Arts Centre), which was built 1776, would later be used as the Town Hall.

In the aftermath of the 1798 Rebellion and the passing of the Act of Union two years later, the landed gentry funded new public buildings including courthouses, in part as an expression of control and authority. The Wexford grand jurors pro-

The Tholsel building and fish market in the Bullring, photographed in 1896.

posed to build a new assize courthouse on the quay, directly facing the old wooden Wexford Bridge – the scene of slaughter by both sides during the rebellion. The location at the time was known as Custom House Quay, later identified as Wellington Quay on the 1840 ordnance survey map and known today as Commercial Quay. The site was owned by John Redmond (great-grandfather of the politician of the same name, who became leader of the Irish Parliamentary Party in 1900). Redmond's brother Walter, who had fought on the side of the British in 1798, regularly sat on the county grand jury.

The county-based grand jury system was the backbone of Irish local government outside of Dublin. The assize courts not only heard the more serious criminal cases but also decided on the taxes to be levied on each county to cover the cost of roads and public services. They were presided over by a travelling judge within a certain 'circuit' and were held twice a year – in spring and summer. A grand jury, made up of twenty-three of the local male elite, was appointed by the High Sheriff of each county.

Cork-born Richard Morrison, a former architectural student of James Gandon, was commissioned in 1802 to design the new Wexford Courthouse, which was completed in 1808. Morrison was also responsible for new courthouses built between 1798 and 1817 in Carlow, Clonmel, Dundalk, Galway, Maryborough (Portlaoise), Naas and Roscommon. Portraits of the then monarch, George III, and of William of Orange were commissioned

Wexford Courthouse, circa. 1900. One of the two roundels is visible above the entrance, the portraits of King George III and William of Orange having been removed. (photo: NLI)

by the grand jury to be included in roundels above the portico of the Wexford Courthouse – reminders of their own sectarian inclinations. However, with the social change in the country brought about by the granting of Catholic Emancipation in 1829, these were painted over during renovations in the 1860s.

A COURT REPORT FROM 1845

'Baron Pennefather entered the court at precisely at ten o'clock', reported

Judge Richard Pennefather (1773-1859).

The Wexford Independent on 9 July 1845, in an account of the proceedings of the previous Friday's quarterly session in Wexford Courthouse. Quarterly sessions acted as the higher criminal court in Ireland outside Dublin, held periodically until 1924. Persons accused of serious criminal offences would first come before the petty sessions courts, which would decide if there was sufficient evidence to justify a trial. If such evidence existed, the magistrate would issue a bill of indictment and refer the matter to a grand jury, which would decide if the bill was correct and supported by evidence, issuing an indictment.

Judge Richard Pennefather was born in Co. Tipperary in 1773. His father William was an MP for Cashel. Richard was appointed King's Counsel in 1816 and served on the Irish Court of Exchequer for 38 years, having been appointed a Baron of the Court in 1821. He was held in such high esteem that even when he went blind in later years, he remained on the bench until the age of 86. He eventually retired a few months before his death. One of his brothers, Edward, was also a distinguished barrister and judge.

The judge opened the proceedings on 4 July 1845 by congratulating the grand jury on the state of the county, having read the court calendar. 'There were only five cases for trial, and one only that required any observation', reported the newspaper. 'Their county appeared to be in that high state of morality and enviable condition, that every other part of the Empire might aspire to, and he trusted that the County of Wexford would long continue to furnish that proud example of peace and tranquility which she now presented.'

Before discharging the grand jury, the judge drew their attention to the current overcrowding of the detention centres for petty offenders in Gorey and Enniscorthy and ordered that 'they should be constructed as not to injure the health of the unfortunate persons that might be placed therein.'

The first defendant to come before Judge Pennefather was Peter Brien, who was accused of murdering James Cummins with a hatchet at Coolamain, Oylegate. A jury was sworn in to hear the case. Addressing the jury, the judge told them that it had been intimated to him that Brien was insane. He said that they therefore needed to decide if the accused stood 'mute of malice or by visitation of God'. Dr. Boxwell, the prison doctor, gave evidence of observing Brien for the past five months in jail. He believed that he was insane prior to his committal and his mental condition had since deteriorated. 'He speaks rationally about his trade, but when spoken to on the subject, on which he is monomaniacal, his jealousy towards his wife, he gets quite insane,' said the doctor. 'What is the district lunatic asylum?' asked the judge. 'Carlow, my Lord,' replied Dr. Boxwell. The jury returned the verdict: 'we find the prisoner, in consequence of being of unsound mind, stands mute of malice.' Judge Pennefather declared: 'Let the prisoner be taken to the Carlow District Lunatic Asylum.'

Next up was Thomas Moulds. He was accused of the manslaughter of Samuel Cornock in Ferns. The first witness called was Dr. John Taylor, a surgeon at Ferns Dispensary, who had examined Cornock on 25 January. He found a tumour close to his navel and was told that he had not received any injury. Dr. Taylor visited him daily and thought he was improving. He believed that he would recover and made his last visit on 10 February. However, the tumour reappeared on 11 March and Cornock had fluid in his abdomen. He deteriorated and eventually died on 24 June.

Dr. Taylor carried out a post-mortem on the body of Samuel Cornock on the day of his death. He concluded that the cause of death was inflammation of the membrane that lines the abdomen and intestines. He explained that a kick or blow would cause the same result, but believed that the injury in this case resulted from external causes.

The deceased's grandmother, Catherine Pepper, told the court that Samuel began working for the accused's father, Valentine Moulds, in December. She said that 'he went in good health and came home in bad health.' A second witness, Catherine Magee, said she visited Cornock on the day before he died. She said a certain woman came in and said: 'Samuel, Samuel, I am sorry to see you dying.' Cornock replied: 'I am not dying yet.' The judge ordered the jury to acquit.

Next up was James Tallon, accused of stealing a pair of 'inexpressibles' [trousers] and of being a vagabond. Police constable James Clingin said he had arrested the defendant after he attempted to enter the home of a Mr Galavan in New Ross by breaking a window. He said that Tallon was *hic et ubique* [here and everywhere] – which caused laughter in the courtroom. He described him as *ignis fatuus* [misleading] 'and could blind all the police under Colonel Macgregor by the light of his countenance, that he was a peripatetic and was fond of being on foot' – which drew ever more laughter. A second policeman stated that Tallon had told him he had no place of residence. At this, the accused cried out: 'What d—d gammon you are going on with – give me a twelve-month or seven years!' The governor of Carlow Prison confirmed that he had him in custody and claimed that he 'pretended to be disturbed in mind.' Judge Pennefather sentenced him to one month in jail and said 'if he did not find security to keep the peace before the expiration of that time, to be transported for seven years.' The final case involved Eliza Maguire who was accused of larceny. She was sentenced to transportation for seven years. 'That concluded the day's proceedings.'

A view of the quays and courthouse in 1892. It was gutted in an IRA arson attack in 1921. (photo: NLI)

In order to relieve the prisons and prison ships in Britain and Ireland, transportation to penal colonies in Australia was the preferred sentence. Transportation numbers from Britain and Ireland dwindled in the 1850s and officially ceased in 1868. Grand juries were replaced with County Councils following the Local Government (Ireland) Act 1898. Wexford County Council held its meetings in Wexford Courthouse between 1899 and 1920.

In June 1921, the courthouse was gutted in an arson attack by the IRA during the War of Independence (1919-21). Francis Carty was with the 4th Battalion of the South Wexford Brigade. He lived above the family shop on North Main Street, within 50 yards of the courthouse. Carty mobilized eight men for the operation. He and accomplice Gerry O'Brien entered the courthouse through a window and emptied six cans of petrol throughout the entire building. They exited and flung paraffin torches through the windows, causing an enormous explosion. Most of the building was destroyed and never rebuilt. A new courthouse was later constructed within the grounds of the jail on Spawell Road in 1930.

WEXFORD JAIL

Mary's Lane (then known as Bride Lane) was the location of a jail in 1656 but shortly after was moved to the 15th century Stafford's Castle on South Main Street, between Stonebridge and Oyster Lane. Hangings were carried out on Windmill Hill (Belvedere Road). The castle continued to operate as a prison for about the next 150 years until a new county jail was built at the junction of Spawell Road and Hill Street in 1812, four years after the completion of the courthouse. The old castle was used as a workhouse until 1845, when the purpose-built Wexford Workhouse opened (this was Wexford County Hospital between 1928 and 1992). Stafford's Castle was finally demolished in the 1880s and a terrace of houses and shops was built on the site.

Wexford Jail's perimeter wall was over 20 feet high. Between 1843 and 1846 an additional fifty-cell block, designed by John Semple, was added. Semple was also responsible for the new façade, which was erected at the same time. The gateway, complete with battlements, also acted as a residence for the gatekeeper. Public executions were carried out on the square outside the entrance gate. The last public hanging took place in 1863 (see page 127) and the last hanging behind prison walls was carried out in 1892.

Wexford Jail, closed in 1903, became St. Brigid's home for inebriated women.
(Tuskar Series postcard published by F. Carty, Wexford)

By the end of the 19th century there was a move to reduce the number of prisons in Ireland. Wexford Jail ceased to function as a prison in 1903 and was acquired by Wexford County Council two years later. The Sisters of St. John of God moved into the complex and ran it as St. Bridgid's – a home for inebriated women. Following the War of Independence, the Irish Free State used it as an army barracks from 1921. Three young anti-Treaty prisoners, Jim Parle, Jack Creane and Pat Hogan, were executed by firing squad outside the old women's prison building in 1923, just a month before the ceasefire that ended the Civil War was declared. The old jail continued to be used as a military barracks until 1931, when it became the headquarters for Wexford County Council. Wexford District Court was also located here. With many modifications carried out over the years, the women's block and entrance are all that remains of the original prison complex. The county council relocated to its new County Hall headquarters at Carricklawn in 2011. Today the site houses the Centre for Irish Research, in partnership with Georgia Southern University, USA.

The old women's prison block on Hill Street is all that remains of the original prison buildings.
(photo: Des Kiely)

Baking 'the staff of life' in Wexford for six generations

Employees of Frank O'Connor & Co. in the 1920s in front of the bakery's Ford Model 4T delivery van. Front row, second left, is Peter Hore, father of Wexford photographer, Ger Hore. (photo: courtesy O'Connor family)

FRANK O'CONNOR & CO., established in 1860, operated its bakery on Wexford's North Main Street for 120 years. Today, the sixth generation of the family continues to supply bread – *'Still the Staff of Life'* – as the front of their building proudly proclaims. The mainstay of the human diet, bread is considered the support of life. The mosaic floor of the shop, laid in 1916 and still to be seen today, includes the inscription: *'Established by Mr & Mrs M.J. O'Connor 1860.'*

In 1856, there were twenty-four outlets on the Main Street baking bread. Before the industrialization of breadmaking and the introduction of the mass-produced sliced pan, shoppers had their favourite local bakery, and O'Connor's grew to be one of Wexford's most popular.

It was founded by Michael Joseph O'Connor at 54 North Main Street in 1860. Michael was born in Wexford in 1835 and married Curracloe girl, Johanna, in Castlebridge in 1863. Michael was a rate collector for Wexford Corporation (perhaps not a popular post to hold). His father, also Michael,

The bakery shop at 54 North Main Street circa 1900, before expansion into the adjoining properties. (photo: Robert French, NLI)

and uncle Timothy were in the building trade. Following Tim's early death, his wife, Mary became a well-known building contractor in her own right.

The North Main Street premises were rather small, with living accommodation on the two upper floors. In 1868, the O'Connors purchased the adjoining property to accommodate their expanding family and business. They had thirteen children – a 'baker's dozen' – all living upstairs, though two died in infancy.

When the family grew older, Michael Joseph and Johanna went to live in 'Weston' on Spawell Road. The running of the bakery was handed over to their son Frank (1877-1909), their fifth born, who traded under the name Frank O'Connor Bakery. Frank was very active in the community during his short 32 years. He was a town councillor and a strong supporter of John Redmond, leader of the Irish Parliamentary Party and advocate of Home Rule. He proposed the motion that Redmond be conferred with the Freedom of the Borough of Wexford. This was effected in 1907, two years before Franks's passing. He was also a volunteer with Wexford Fire Brigade and a member of the Harbour Boat Club, the local Drama Society, St Iberius Club and the Catholic Young Men's Society.

Franks's brother, Michael James, took over the running of the bakery business. M.J. was married to Catherine Wickham from Ballymore in North

Wexford. They had three children: James, Joan and Fintan. The bakery would in turn pass to Fintan. Both M.J. and Fintan became solicitors.

In the early days, all the baking was done by hand in two peel ovens: fixed hearths of brick on which the loaves were placed with a wooden paddle. The first of two coal-burning Scotch ovens, with two large drawplates on metal tracks, was installed in 1910. Deliveries of flour came mainly from Davis Flour Mills in Enniscorthy. As the business expanded, larger ovens were added and in about 1918 the bakery converted to gas. A Crossley gas engine was acquired and this worked off town gas and the bakery was then known as a steam bakery. The gas was fed from the Wexford Gas Company works on Trinity Street where, from 1865, gas and tar were produced from burning coal, and stored. This site was recently occupied by C&D Hardware.

As well as bread, O'Connor's baked exceptional cakes for birthdays, weddings and Christmas. Their chocolate roll was legendary in Wexford town and throughout the county. The bakery had a fleet of four horse-drawn delivery vans. The main stables were at Stratham's in Westgate. One of the carts is currently on public display in the Irish Agricultural Museum in Johnstown Castle. Frank O'Connor's Model Steam Bakery was the first bakery in the town to have motorized transport when the horses were replaced.

Adjoining premises were acquired and the business was extended onto Commercial Quay and the Bullring. The former John Daly shop on the corner of the Bullring was demolished and in 1923 the O'Connors opened the fondly-remembered Ritz Café.

James O'Connor, the sixth generation of the family to carry on business in the town, is the great-great grandson of Michael Joseph O'Connor who started the original bakery in 1860. In the centenary year of 1960, the shop was enlarged and developed into a fine self-service supermarket, the first in Wexford. It was based on the early Connolly's Supermarket in Dún Laoghaire. James began work in the bakery at the age of 13, wrapping bread and cakes by hand. He later worked in the fruit and vegetable

The old entrance on Commercial Quay to Frank O'Connor's Bakery. (photo: Paddy Donovan)

John Daly bakery and provisions shop at 52 North Main Street was acquired by the O'Connor family.

Having demolished and rebuilt the old Daly building in 1923, the O'Connors opened the popular Ritz Café on the corner of the Bullring.

business, taking Wexford produce to be sold in the Dublin markets and returning with products to the shops and restaurants of Wexford. He started married life living above the shop on North Main Street, and after the bakery closed in 1980 the business evolved into the fresh-food hall, delicatessen and later wine merchants known as Greenacres.

Thomas Ryan, for many years manager of Frank O'Connor & Company, purchased much of the bakery equipment when it closed. Since 1984, he has operated his own enterprise using the same recipes, and Ryan's Bakery continues to supply its bread to Wexford and surrounding counties.

The widowed aunt of Michael Joseph O'Connor, the original founder of the bakery, was Mary (née McGuire) O'Connor (1837-1927). She had been married to his uncle Timothy, a building contractor. Her own father, Hugh McGuire, was a ship chandler and three times Mayor of Wexford from 1892-4. Timothy was a renowned builder of the time. Having been engaged in the refurbishment of the Franciscan Friary in Wexford, he was working on the roof of the Friary in Waterford when he caught pneumonia. He died in the city in 1881 aged 40, leaving his widow and five very young children, all aged under ten.

Mary had run her own small private school on the site now occupied by the Talbot Hotel and a chinaware shop on North Main Street. Following her husband's passing, she very successfully carried on his construction business and became a formidable businesswoman.

One of the first buildings completed by Mary O'Connor, known as 'The Builder', was the convent chapel for the St John of God sisters on Newtown Road. Timothy had built the convent itself. Mary was

Mary O'Connor (1837-1927), known as 'The Builder', had many of Wexford's iconic buildings constructed.

also responsible for the construction of the impressive convent for the Adoration sisters adjacent to Bride Street Church, which was begun in 1885. In 1890, she had an extension added to the convent of the Presentation sisters on Francis Street. Mary was responsible for the construction of the terrace of three-storey houses on Upper George's Street, Glena Terrace on Spawell Road, nearby Ard Ruadh House as well as residential and commercial properties on Wexford's Main Street. In 1909, she was contracted to build a pavilion at Rosslare Golf Club. However the entire building was washed away by the sea in the 1940s and 50s.

One of Mary O'Connor's most accomplished structures is the redbrick office building on the corner of Lower George's Street and Selskar Street. She had it built in 1894 for her grand-nephews, James and Michael James O'Connor, for their legal practice. It was the site of the former townhouse of the barrister, Beauchamp Bagenal Harvey of Bargy Castle, who was executed for his part in the 1798 Rising. Mary died in 1927 aged 90 at Glena Terrace, in one of the eight striking terraced houses that she had built in 1890-5.

Today, the terrace is occupied by another member of the family, solicitor Catherine O'Connor. Having joined the M.J. O'Connor firm in 1995, Catherine

The former M.J. O'Connor Solicitors office building on the corner of Lower George's Street and Selskar Street. It was constructed by the building contactor Mrs Mary O'Connor in 1894 on the site of the former townhouse of the barrister and 1798 rebel leader, Bagenal Harvey. (photo: Des Kiely)

set up the law firm, O'Connor Mullen, in partnership with Cormac Mullen in 2017 at 1 Glena Terrace.

In 1900, James, aged 28, left the legal practice after being called to the Irish Bar, and quickly rose in his profession. He was appointed Solicitor-General in 1914, Attorney-General in 1917 and a Supreme Court judge in 1918. James actively pursued a peaceful settlement to the War of Independence, informally meeting opposing leaders in London, but without success. Following the establishment of the Irish Free State, he moved to England. He was called to the English Bar and knighted in 1925. Sir James returned to Wexford and rejoined the family firm, but died soon after in 1931.

Michael James was apprenticed to Martin Huggard before becoming a very successful solicitor in Wexford. M.J. O'Connor Solicitors were heavily involved in the purchase of land by tenants after the passing of the Land Purchase Act of 1888. M.J. was a strong advocate of tenants' rights and the firm completed the controversial sale of John Redmond's estate following Redmond's death in 1918.

M.J.'s son Fintan was born in 1900. He became an apprentice to his father in 1917 and qualified as a solicitor in 1923, having graduated from Trinity College. A great raconteur who enjoyed shooting wildfowl in the North and South Slobs, he was known in the firm as 'The Boss'. Fintan was a highly polished and accomplished court advocate and spent 56 years in the practice, up to 1979.

After 110 years occupying the historic building on Selskar Street, the solicitors' firm moved to a newly-built office building in Drinagh in 2004. The listed building now forms part of Green Acres delicatessen, wine merchants, restaurant and art gallery. It is operated by James O'Connor, the sixth generation of the family to carry on business in the town. He and his wife Paula moved the business from North Main Street to the M.J. O'Connor Solicitors building in 2005 and later added a large contemporary glass extension. A bakery was established on the top floor in 2013, continuing the family baking tradition.

In 2020, James and Paula O'Connor, together with their son Patrick, reopened the North Main Street former bakery that still retains the initials *FOC* above the entrance. James named it 'Frank's Place' after his great-granduncle, the fifth child of the original baker's dozen, who contributed so much to the community in his short life.

James Joyce immortalized the Wexford family in *Ulysses*, his novel set in 1904 Dublin. From *Episode Ten – Wandering Rocks*: '*He followed his guest to the outlet and then whirled his lath away among the pillars. With J.J. O'Molloy he came forth slowly into Mary's abbey where draymen were loading floats with sacks of carob and palm nut meal, O'Connor, Wexford.*'

Grateful thanks to James O'Connor for his assistance in compiling this story.

The 'Dutch Billy' façade on North Main Street was remodelled in a more ornate style and the words 'Bread is Still the Staff of Life' added. Frank O'Connor's Bakery was renamed Greenacres. (photo: James O'Connor)

Bibliography

Books

Butler, Richard, *Building the Irish Courthouse and Prison* (Cork, 2020)

Colfer, Billy, *The Hook Peninsula* (Cork, 2004)

Doyle, Ian (Ed.) and Browne, Bernard (Ed.), *Medieval Wexford* (Dublin, 2016)

Enright, Michael, *Men of Iron* (Wexford, 1987)

Gaffney, Phyllis, *Healing Amid the Ruins* (Dublin, 2000)

Hore, Philip Herbert, *History of the Town and County of Wexford* (London, 1900-11)

McMenamin, Marc, *Codebreaker* (Dublin, 2018)

Milne, Ida, *Stacking the Coffins* (Manchester, 2020)

O'Malley, Ernie, *The Singing Flame* (Cork, 2012)

Raftery, D. and Kilbride, C., *The Benedictine Nuns and Kylemore Abbey* (Newbridge, 2020)

Shepherd, Ernie, *Fishguard & Rosslare Railways & Harbours Company* (Newtownards, 2015)

Newspapers

Enniscorthy Guardian

Freeman's Journal

Gorey Guardian

Inishowen Independent

Irish Press

Irish Times

New Ross Standard

Wexford Free Press

Wexford Herald

Wexford Independent

Wexford People

Other sources

British Library

Bureau of Military History, Dublin

Chronicling America

Dictionary of Irish Biography

Dúchas/National Folklore Collection

History Ireland

Irish Historical Studies

Library Ireland

National Inventory of Architectural Heritage

National Library of Ireland (NLI)

National Library of Australia

National Museums Northern Ireland

RTÉ Archives

University of Notre Dame, USA

Wexford County Archive

Wexford County Library

Printed in Great Britain
by Amazon

27913113R00124